Saturn:
the Reaper

BY

ALAN LEO

Being the substance of a Course of PUBLIC LECTURES *delivered before the* ASTROLOGICAL SOCIETY, *in the months of January, February and March*, 1916.

WITH AN INTRODUCTION

"*Be not deceived, God is not mocked,*
whatsoever a man soweth that shall he also reap"

SAMUEL WEISER
New York
1973

SYNOPSIS

SAMUEL WEISER INC.
734 Broadway
New York, N. Y. 10003

ISBN 0-87728-019-3
Library of Congress Card No. 75-16450

Printed in U.S.A. by
NOBLE OFFSET PRINTERS, INC.
New York, N.Y. 10003

FOREWORD

THE fool has said in his heart "There is no God." And the astrologer, going to the other extreme, has declared that there are many gods, each subject to the One Supreme Power—Almighty God—Whose Will they know *how* to obey.

The three lectures recently given before the Astrological Society and now published in these pages were mainly concerned with that one of the great Gods, or Spiritual Intelligences, whose physical planet is known to us under the name of SATURN. Many names have been given to the Being who presides over this planetary sphere, but none of them conveys so much meaning as that of "Saturn," GOD OF JUSTICE, whose mission it is to chastise and purify the souls of men through pain and suffering. For although familiarly termed by the student of Astrology a "malefic" influence, he is also known as the god of Contemplation, Regeneration and Perfection.

ASTROLOGY, rightly understood, reveals a law that is ever working to further human progress. During the early stages of his evolution Man is compelled to learn certain necessary lessons; *compelled*, for at the beginning of his evolution he is not master of his fate or destiny. But as he learns to work with Nature, and to control the vehicles with which Nature has supplied him, and through which his consciousness is working, he becomes a coöperator with Nature and uses her unchanging laws to unfold his own hitherto concealed spiritual, or real, Self.

Truth reveals itself to each individual in a different way. The Sun shines equally upon all; the crystal reflects the light back to the Sun but less so the clod of earth. Truth is the result of real experience, and does not consist in the transfer of intellectual symbols from one person to another. Symbology may convey many hints concerning precious knowledge to a soul ready for such knowledge, but personal exertion or study is the only means by which real progress can be achieved.

The writer has made a careful and sincere study of Astrology for nearly thirty years, and has tested his studies by first-hand experience lasting over a quarter of a century. Although he realises that the fruit of his labours can only be appreciated by the few in this century, when the pursuit of the material is only *beginning* to yield to a desire for and search after Truth, he is content to work for a future generation whose eyes will more easily discern the spiritual than does the present generation, bewildered as it is by the changing world about it.

May these lectures prove helpful and useful to those sufficiently awake to understand them, those who have begun to glimpse something of the great truth that

CHARACTER IS DESTINY.

"*Nothing but such certainty can quiet our revolted sense of justice. For, when one unacquainted with the noble doctrine looks around him, and observes the inequalities of birth and fortune, of intellect and capacities; when one sees honour paid to fools and profligates, on whom fortune has heaped her favours by mere privilege of birth, and their nearest neighbour, with all his intellect and noble virtues—far more deserving in every way—perishing of want and for lack of sympathy; when one sees all this and has to turn away, helpless to relieve the undeserved suffering, one's ears ringing and heart aching with the cries of pain around him—that blessed knowledge of Karma alone prevents him from cursing life and men, as well as their supposed Creator.*"

"*Secret Doctrine*" ii, 317.

"*Yes; our destiny* IS *written in the stars! . . . This is not superstition, least of all is it fatalism. . . . It is now amply proved that even horoscopes and judiciary astrology are not quite based on fiction, and that Stars and Constellations, consequently, have an occult and mysterious influence on, and connection with, individuals. And if with the latter, why not with nations, races, and mankind as a whole?*"

Ibid i, 700, 709.

INTRODUCTION

THE true astrologer does not view individuals as distinct and isolated entities placed side by side, but as the varied manifestations of *ONE* unchanging universal consciousness. The Sun he considers to be the physical glory of the Lord of the Solar Universe, radiating the Universal Consciousness throughout this solar system. As light from a single source produces the appearance of different lights by reflection from a number of surfaces, so this universal consciousness, while itself remaining unchanged, produces endless individualities, which in the course of their evolution reach perfection by recognising this essential unity.

The astrologer further views the planetary spheres as being each a centre of a *specialised* consciousness, each with its own definite rays of influence which individuals absorb and 'temper' in themselves, producing what are known as the special "temperaments." These planetary spheres of influence are not concerned with humanity alone but with other departments of Nature also, over which they have special, though not exclusive or isolated control. For instance the planetary sphere of Saturn is largely concerned with the crystallisations of the Mineral Kingdom; and in this idea the modern astrologer sees the rationale of the ancient astrologer's statement, handed down through many centuries, that Saturn governs the bony structure in man and his concrete or scientific mind.

Astrology is one, though after all only one, of the languages seeking to express the truth about man, his origin, nature and destiny, as well as his relations to the surrounding world of objects. Through Astrology we may acquire Wisdom. Wisdom is a change in the quality of our consciousness, it is not merely a surface expansion of it, and although the symbology of Astrology may be eminently useful it is not in itself spiritual knowledge, and never can be converted into it until it is "inwardly digested."

Astrology proves, with undeniable certainty, that no two individuals can be exactly alike, whether physically or otherwise. Spiritual food, on assimilation, whether by means of the philosophy of Astrology or through the religions of the nations, partakes of the peculiarities of the individual. The "I" in each of us is an individuality of consciousness, and through Astrology we learn that each "I" or individuality is immortal, as it is a unit of the one eternal principle. Just as the ocean as a whole is salt so is every separate drop ocean salt, and each "I" is the salt of the earth clothed in three bodies—a physical body, an emotional body and a body of thought; any or all of which bodies may change, but the essence of the "I" in each individual never.

If the individual consciousness in each of us is indestructible, and Astrology shows why it must be, then it is worth our while to trace our relationship to one or other of the great spheres of influence presided over by the spiritual Intelligences. Our relations to matter are constantly changing in answer to a definite law. Astrology has ever taught the constant change in the relations of the earth, the moon and the stars. Life is nothing but a constant change, and the products of the change are bound to each other in a very definite manner. We know that everything is related to that which has already transpired. Our experiences are based on this constant change, and from this we learn that without the law of causation, our experiences, either mental or physical, would be impossible. We may trace our experiences of pleasure and pain in the present to causes generated in the past, and those astrologers who are spiritually minded believe most emphatically that whatever we sow we must also reap.

The true astrologer may hopefully interpret his science or philosophy in this wise, which is but the law of action and reaction ensuring that of necessity we reap what we have sown.

The interpretations of Astrology are perfectly logical. If individual consciousness is immortal, and its experiences are governed by this law of action and reaction, then it follows that so long as all causes capable of producing effects on the present plane of life are not exhausted, and the generation of similar causes is not stopped, the individual consciousness will remain connected with the experiences of earthly existence. This opens up the whole question of the soul's re-embodiment or re-incarnation, and although Astrology as an experimental science is not vitally affected either by a belief or disbelief in this theory, it supports it more strongly than any other science or philosophy.

The fundamental belief of the real Astrology is that there is a principle of consciousness in man which is immortal, and that this principle was derived by man at the birth of his soul from one of the Spiritual Intelligences who preside over the physical planets in our solar system, since they are the Creative Principles in that system.

From this it follows that this principle is manifested many times on earth until earth's experiences have been exhausted, and the experiences of the different incarnations are strictly governed by the law of causation. The idea opens up a vast field of enquiry, and shows that each individual is the result of a distinct causal necessity in Nature.

In this age when the ruling powers of certain nations are seeking to call out the martial spirit in a great number of individuals, it may be well to state that Astrology distinctly proves that it is not wise for any man to dominate the life and action of another, no matter what their relative stages of development may be.

There is an absolute unity in Nature, which is eternal; and we are all parts of one great whole, evolving under a clearly defined plan written in the heavens, which he who runs may read. The wise man rules his stars by seeing that as a unit he must seek to harmonise himself first with his stars and then with the Sun which is the source of all light and also of life which is light.

Astrology is the most hopeful teaching the world has ever known. It establishes a firm belief in the unchanging law. It reveals the truth with regard to our immortality and shows us why we must reap what we have sown.

Christ, the spiritual teacher of our race, said "In my Father's house are many mansions." He also exhorted us to be perfect even as our Father in heaven is perfect. Saturn is one of the Fathers in heaven, and he will see that none pass his purifying influence who are not truly perfect in thought, word and deed. He is also Father Time who prepares for Eternity.

THE FOUR BOOKS OF CLAUDIUS PTOLEMY

Astrology is mistakenly supposed to have received its death blow when Copernicus propounded what is now accepted as the true system of the universe, although, as every student of astrology knows, the science was and could be in no way affected by the revelation of the fact (already known and taught by Pythagoras) that the Sun was the centre of the solar system and not the earth; since Astrology deals with the *relative* positions of the planets, which may be determined by observation and are therefore not affected by a change in astronomical theories designed to account for them. We are consequently able to profit by the labours of astrologers of the past, and Ptolemy did our present students a great service through his "Tetrabiblos" or Quadripartite, the four books of the influence of the stars, a work which has received many translations, the last and perhaps the best being a translation by J. Ashmand from the Greek paraphrase of Proclus published in 1822.

It will be instructive, and will form a useful conclusion to this Introduction, to consider what is there set down regarding Saturn.

From Ptolemy we learn that Saturn was always considered a cold planet, for he says in the fourth chapter of Book I. that "Saturn produces cold and dryness, for he is most remote both from the Sun's heat and from the earth's vapours. But he is more effective in the production of cold than of dryness. And he and the rest of the planets derive their energy from the positions which they hold with regard to the Sun and Moon; and they are all seen to alter the constitution of the Ambient in various ways." He also says in the following chapter that "Saturn and Mars are esteemed of a contrary nature, and malefic, or causers of evil:—the first from his excess of cold, the other from his excess of dryness."

In Chapter 21 we are told that Saturn rules Aquarius by day and Capricorn by night, and it also governs the east wind.

Saturn as Sole Governor

In Book II., Chapter 9, Ptolemy explains the nature of Saturn by saying that "when Saturn may be the sole governor, he will produce disasters concomitant with cold. And in so far as the event may apply to the human race in particular, it will induce among men lingering diseases, consumptions, declines, rheumatisms, disorders from watery humours, and attacks of the quartan ague; as well as exile, poverty, and a general mass of evils, griefs, and alarms: deaths also will be frequent, but chiefly among persons advanced in age. That part of the brute creation which is most serviceable to man will likewise suffer, and be destroyed by disease;

and men who make use of the animals thus diseased will be infected by them, and perish with them. The atmosphere will become dreadfully chill and frosty, unwholesome, turbid and gloomy, presenting only clouds and pestilence. Copious and destructive storms of snow and hail will descend, generating and fostering insects and reptiles noxious to mankind. In rivers, and at sea, tempests will be frequent and general, causing disastrous voyages and many shipwrecks; and even fish will be destroyed. The waters of the sea will retire for a time, and again return and produce inundations; rivers will overflow their banks, and cause stagnant pools; and the fruits of the earth, especially such as are necessary to sustain life, will be lost and cut off by blight, locusts, floods, rains, hail, or some similar agency; and the loss will be so extensive as to threaten even famine."

In Book III., Chapter 16, describing the form and temperament of the body, Ptolemy says "Saturn, when oriental, acts on the personal figure by producing a yellowish complexion and a good constitution; with black and curled hair, a broad and stout chest, eyes of ordinary quality, and a proportionate size of body, the temperament of which is compounded principally of moisture and cold. Should he be occidental, he makes the personal figure black or dark, thin and small, with scanty hair on the head; the body without hair, but well shaped; the eyes black or dark; and the bodily temperament consisting chiefly of dryness and cold."

Influence on the Mind

In the same Book, Chapter 18, dealing with the quality of the mind, it is stated that the planet Saturn, "when alone possessing dominion of the mind, and governing Mercury and the Moon, and if posited in glory, both cosmically and with respect to the angles, will make men careful of their bodies, strong and profound in opinion, austere, singular in their modes of thinking, laborious, imperious, hostile to crime, avaricious, parsimonious, accumulators of wealth, violent, and envious; but, if he be not in glory, cosmically, and as regards the angles, he will debase the mind, making it penurious, pusillanimous, ill-disposed, indiscriminating, malignant, timorous, slanderous, fond of solitude, repining, incapable of shame, bigoted, fond of labour, void of natural affection, treacherous in friendship and in family connections, incapable of enjoyment, and regardless of the body.

"Connected with Jupiter in the mode before mentioned, being also situated in glory, Saturn will render the mind virtuous, respectful, well-intentioned, ready to assist, judicious, frugal, magnanimous, obliging, solicitous of good, affectionate in all domestic ties, mild, prudent, patient, and philosophical: but, if thus connected and posited ingloriously, he makes men outrageous, incapable of learning, timorous, highly superstitious, yet regardless of religion, suspicious, averse to children, incapable of friendship, cunning, misjudging, faithless, foolishly wicked, irascible, hypocritical, idle and useless, without ambition, yet regretful, morose, highly reserved, over-cautious and dull.

"Conciliated with Mars, and posited in glory, Saturn renders men reckless, over-diligent, free in speech, turbulent, boastful, austere in their dealings, pitiless, contemptuous, fierce, warlike, bold, fond of tumults, insidious, deceitful, and implacable ; promoters of faction, tyrannical, rapacious, hostile to the commonwealth, delighting in strife, vindictive, profound in guilt, strenuous, impatient, insolent, mischievous, over-bearing, evil, unjust, obstinate, inhuman, inflexible, immutable in opinion, busy, able in office, active, submitting to no opposition, and on the whole successful in their undertakings ; but, if thus connected, and not placed in glory, he will make men plunderers, robbers, adulterers, submissive to evil, seeking gain by their turpitude, infidels in religion, void of common affections, mischievous, treacherous, thievish, perjurers, and sanguinary; eaters of unlawful food, familiar with guilt, assassins, sorcerers, sacrilegious, impious, violators of the tomb, and, in short, thoroughly depraved.

"Conciliated with Venus, and being again in glory, Saturn makes men averse to women, and renders them fond of governing, prone to solitude, highly reserved, regardless of rank, indifferent to beauty, envious, austere, unsociable, singular in opinion, addicted to divination and to religious services and mysteries; solicitous to the priesthood, fanatical, and subservient to religion; solemn, reverential, sedate, studious of wisdom, faithful in friendship, continent, reflective, circumspect, and scrupulous in regard to female virtue: but, if he be thus conciliated, and not posited in glory, he makes men licentious and libidinous, practisers of lewdness, careless and impure in sexual intercourse; obscene, treacherous to women, especially to those of their own families; wanton, quarrelsome, sordid, hating elegance; slanderous, drunken, superstitious, adulterous, and impious; blasphemers of the gods, and scoffers at holy rights; calumniators, sorcerers, hesitating at nothing.

"If conciliated with Mercury, and if in a glorious position, Saturn makes men inquisitive, loquacious, studious of law and of medicine, mystical, confederate in secrecy, fabricators of miracles, impostors, improvident, cunning, familiar with business, quick in perception, petulant, accurate, vigilant, meditative, fond of employment, tractable: but, if connected with Mercury, and not posited gloriously, he causes men to be frivolous, vindictive, laborious, alienated from their families, fond of tormenting, and void of enjoyment; night-wanderers, insidious, treacherous, pitiless, and thievish; magicians, sorcerers, forgers of writings, cheats, unsuccessful in their undertakings, and quickly reduced to adversity.—Such are the effects of Saturn."

Fortune and Employment

In Book IV., Chapter 2, concerning the fortune of wealth, it is said that "Saturn will effect the acquirement of wealth by means of buildings, agriculture, or navigation. . . . Should Saturn, however, when thus in influence over the fortune of wealth, be also configurated with Jupiter, he particularly provides wealth through inheritance; especially if the configuration should exist in superior angles."

Chapter 4 dealing with the quality of employment says of Saturn that when bearing testimony jointly with Mercury, "persons then born will become managers of the affairs of others, or interpreters of dreams, or will be engaged in temples for the purposes of divination, and for the sake of their fanaticism." The joint influence of Saturn connected with the planets seems to add gravity, and in some cases, dignity to the employment.

In Chapter 9, dealing with the kind of death, we learn that Saturn "will produce death by means of lingering diseases; cough, rheumatism, flux, ague, disorder of the spleen, dropsy, cholic, and complaints in the womb; and in short, by all such diseases as proceed from the super-abundance of cold."

Many other statements are made with regard to the nature of death as shown by the influence of Saturn, and in Chapter 10 dealing with the periodical Divisions of

Time it is stated that "Saturn, moving in the last sphere, regulates the final old age, as agreeing with its chilliness. He obstructs the mental movements, the appetites and enjoyments; rendering them imbecile and dull, in conformity with the dullness of his own motion."

In the Centiloquy, or Hundred Aphorisms of Claudius Ptolemy, the 76th says:—"If Saturn holds the Mid-heaven, and the conditionary luminary be opposed to him, the native will perish in the ruins of buildings, provided the sign of the lower heaven be an earthly sign; if it be a watery sign, he will be drowned or suffocated by water: if a human sign, he will be strangled by men, or will perish by the halter or the scourge. Should there, however, be a benefic in the eighth house, he will not suffer death, although he will be brought near it."

Modern astrologers have accepted the teachings of the Four Books of Ptolemy, and none of them have disagreed with these statements, but have amplified them and extended them as much as their experience and intuition will allow. In the following lectures an elaboration of the influence of Saturn is given based upon the experiences of the author.

"When the time for reincarnation comes, and the presence of the Permanent Atom renders possible the fertilisation of the ovum from which the new body is to grow, its keynote sounds out, and is one of the forces which guide the ethereal builder to choose the material suitable for his work, for he can use none that cannot be to some extent attuned to the permanent atom. But it is only *one* of the forces; the karma of past lives, mental, emotional, and in relation to others, demands materials capable of the most varied expressions; out of that karma the Lords of Karma have chosen such as is congruous, and this congruous mass of karma determines the material group, overriding the permanent atom, and out of that group are chosen by the ethereal builder such materials as can vibrate in harmony with the permanent atom, or in discords not disruptive in their violence. . . . According to this temperament will be the time of the birth of the body; it *must* be born into the world at a time when the physical planetary influences are suitable, and it thus is born under its astrological 'star.' It is not the star that imposes the temperament, but the temperament that fixes the epoch of birth under that star. Herein lies the explanation of the correspondences between Star-Angels and characters, and the usefulness for educational purposes of a skilfully and carefully drawn horoscope as a guide to the personal temperament of a child."

ANNIE BESANT, *A Study in Consciousness* pp. 98-100.

Saturn: The Reaper.

LECTURE I.

SYNOPSIS.—Saturn, The Reaper—Its influence contrasted with that of Mars, the Sower—its individualising influence and relation to the permanent physical atom—its moralising influence and relation to the three last Signs of the Zodiac—why Saturn is the Bridge between the higher and lower Self.

"Mars: the War Lord"

IN the Course of Lectures delivered a year ago, in dealing with the vibrations of the planets in connection with the Great World War, we turned our attention to the influence of MARS, THE WAR LORD,—the Sower, or energiser; tracing that planet's influence from the beginnings of instinctual consciousness through various stages until it was seen to culminate in the highest human point it could reach, that of devotion to an embodied ideal.

We have now in this second Course of Lectures to deal with the far more subtle vibration of Saturn's influence.

The influences of the planets MARS and SATURN are the great extremes in human evolution, giving rise to the greatest complexities in life, and for this reason they are very truly considered in the early stages of our evolution as wholly malefic and inimical to man. The influence of Mars when in affliction plunges him into a fever, and no hell can burn more fiercely than the scorching flame of a self-centred desire-nature; while the influence of Saturn, when in affliction, drives him to extreme states of exclusion and isolation in which he finds himself plunged into the horror of a black despair or into the Arctic night of an appalling despondency. The planets Mars and Saturn are, under certain conditions, the extremes of so-called "evil," but it will be our duty to show that instead of being evil and malefic they are the cause of forces in Nature which are ever affecting involution and evolution, and that they are not only *indispensable* to our human progress, but actual INCENTIVES to that progress, and that we could not make headway without their influence.

MARS and SATURN

All the planetary influences reaching our globe affect us physically, emotionally and intellectually through our physical, astral or emotional, and mental bodies. They are not *directly* concerned with our spiritual unfoldment, although they indirectly lead to that end; and in this statement we have the basis of all

Physical, Emotional, Mental

arguments regarding the problems of fate and free-will. The planet Mars, as already stated in the previous course of lectures, very largely affects the emotional or animal soul in man, this planet's influence being very much concerned with the cerebellum of the brain, the seat of the driving force without which there would be no animal or physical strength. The relation of the planet Mercury to the cerebrum was also pointed out, serving to polish and refine the crude force supplied by the martian influence stored in the cerebellum and base of the brain. And in the same manner that MARS was shown to govern the physical or animal part of Man's nature, we shall now demonstrate that the influence of SATURN stimulates the moral nature or finer qualities of reason, or common sense, in man.

The One aim of Human Destiny

Every human being is essentially a seed of the divine life, and the unfoldment of the spiritual life within him is the one aim of human destiny. This seed is involved, or plunged by involution, into the material worlds, and on reaching the animal kingdom it is stimulated into activity by the direct influence of the planet Mars, which acts as a compelling or *driving* force. On passing upwards out of the animal kingdom into the lowest levels of the human family it is still under the influence of Mars, which acts as an attractive force drawing out the many latent qualities through the desires of flesh, such as hunger for material food, sex craving, desires for physical comforts, pleasures and luxuries of various kinds, which go on actively energising the animal man until he realises the penalties and limitations which prevent a *full* satisfaction of his desire and which eventually lead to sorrow, pain and satiety. It is at THIS point of realisation that the influence of Saturn begins, and it is usually a very long time before the nature of the limiting or resisting power of Saturn is understood.

Centrifugal and Centripetal

It is the natural mission of Mars to project and impel all the latent forces of matter, to push it forward or outward without restraint or hindrance. It is in a word what we may term the centrifugal tendency of our universe and therefore tends to drive the qualities of the "seed" from the centre outward. The influence of Saturn is exactly the reverse, its whole tendency is what may be termed centripetal and tends to draw all things back to a centre. This is the basis of all our *science* of astrology, which considers the planetary influences, collectively, as an expression of the Great Architect of our planetary chain of worlds, whose vibrations are so arranged that one set of influences impels the matter through which the self manifests outwards and another set drives it inwards; and in this respect Mars and Saturn—the influence of both of which is mostly physical and astral—are the great extremes, or what we may term the high water mark of possibilities in the outward and inward directions. This interpretation allows us to discover the same tendencies in all the planets, but with those tendencies polarised differently. It also explains sex peculiarities or the male and female elements, the positive and negative action of planetary influence; and we can see that from a scientific aspect the planetary influences, while affecting us physically and morally, have no immediate concern with the higher principles.

Ebb and Flow

It is the law of nature that all material things shall ebb and flow, and within nature we find two elements which allow for every form of expansion and for all forms of limitation; they may be summed up as representing Space and Time. And we may use these two fundamental conditions of the mind, as the ancient astrologers were wont to do, to express in a scientific manner every tendency it is possible to express, and trace each to one of the seven great planetary influences.

♈ - ♂
♑ - ♄

The circle of the fixed zodiac, the ecliptic,[1] is so generally accepted, having been proved beyond all question by advanced students of astrology to represent, through the ethers of space, the various qualities of matter in all its manifold forms, that we have only to refer to it to discover exactly how far we

---

[1] For relation between this zodiac and the zodiacal Constellations, see Note on the Zodiac, p. xv., *Mars: the War Lord.*

may treat of both Mars and Saturn to discover their apparently opposing influences. Aries, the first sign of the fixed zodiac, is governed by the planet Mars, and in the last course of lectures we dealt very fully with that planet in its relation to the twelve zodiacal signs. We will now deal in the same manner with the planet Saturn in relation to the sign Capricorn and the tenth house of a horoscope.

The zodiac begins, in our present age, with the most expansive of all the twelve signs; and according to the Buddhist teaching with regard to the Nidânas it is the sign of Avidyâ—meaning that a sensible recognition of the universe has not been acquired by the human soul, which is said to enter at this stage upon the wheel or circle of necessity. The sign Aries is symbolised by the Ram, an animal that *butts* its way through obstacles, or forces a course by sheer energy blindly and without deliberation or without exercising a clear and open sight. It is the sign of Cardinal or changeable Fire, signifying constant and rapid movement.

Aries the Ram

We need not pursue these ideas further at present, interesting and instructive though they will prove on closer examination,[2] but we may state that the Nidânas are said to link up sentient existence between subjective

The Nidanas

[2] The Nidânas are fully dealt with in *The Pathway of the Soul*, by J. Henry Van Stone.

and objective natures. The "seed" coming downward into manifestation is involved in a concatenation of causes and effects, and its state is represented by one or other of the Nidânas, which havc a peculiar resemblance to the signs of the zodiac. Both Nidânas and zodiacal signs are related to cause and effect, or Karma, and through them the careful student may follow some of the most intricate laws of Karma.

So far as the actual influence of the planet Mars is concerned, it may be said to begin with the sign Aries and to end with the sign Capricorn, the sign of its exaltation, where the centrifugal or outgoing energies end and the centripetal tendencies begin.

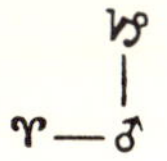

If we note carefully the influence of Saturn with regard to the signs of the zodiac we shall find that the actual influence of Saturn is practically confined to the signs Capricorn and Aquarius, and affects, more exclusively than any other planet, all that these signs represent. The planet Mars dominates, in a very real sense, nominally as over-lord, all the signs from Aries to Scorpio; but it does not dominate, or even influence, to any great extent the last three signs Capricorn, Aquarius and Pisces—the astral impulse, passional fire and force of Mars being reduced or subdued in these signs. Indeed, if the statement is not too metaphysical we may say that for the unregenerate man the first nine signs out of the whole circle of the zodiac give him unlimited scope for the energies of his physical life and offer no permanent or persistent restraint until the sign Capricorn is reached, when restraint and definite restrictions begin. In this respect, however, Sagittarius may be termed a neutral or "stop-gap" sign.

Spring, Summer, Autumn,—

The planet Mars ruling the eastern quarter of the zodiac represents the Springtime of life, the northern angle the Summer, followed by the Autumn in the western angle, and the Winter at the southern angle. The only cure for the fever and heat of Mars is extreme cold. The passional nature of Mars loves the Springtime, glories in the Summer and dreads the Autumn and the Winter; a truly symbolical representation of Mars and the animal man.

WINTER

The sign Capricorn, in common with all the zodiacal signs, has a dual meaning. The goat symbol of Capricorn is more intimately related to the exaltation of Mars in that sign, the true Saturnian symbol for Capricorn is however the crocodile, or to be correct the serpent and the mystical "Dragon," a symbol having the deepest occult meaning. Gerald Massey in *The Natural Genesis* reveals some of this meaning when he shows that the goddess of the Great Bear and Mother of Time was in Egypt from the earliest times the "Living Word," and that "Sevekh-Kronus, whose type was the crocodile-Dragon, the pre-planetary form of Saturn, was called her son and consort; he was her Word—logos: (vol. i, 321; ii, 313).

The crocodile is the Egyptian Dragon. It was the dual symbol of heaven and earth, Sun and Moon, and was sacred, owing its dual nature to both Osiris and Isis. In *The Pathway of the Soul* it is said that Seb, or Saturn, is symbolised by the Goose as a sacred animal, and in the *Book of the Dead* Seb is called the great Cackler who produces the world egg. In the evolution of the soul Saturn is the ruler of the sign Capricorn, wherein is formed the *embryo* of the New Man, and thus the egg becomes an appropriate symbol in the lesser cycle of Man. The egg surrounded by its shell also suggests the limitations of Saturn, the separateness of the self-conscious centre.

Egyptian Symbols

If we now say that Time and Space are personified in the signs Capricorn and Aquarius it must not be taken too literally or we shall not be able to trace the wide difference between the abstract nature of Saturn and the concrete influence of Mars. Saturn is both the most abstract and yet the most concrete influence of the zodiac. Concrete when wholly identified with the *circle* of the zodiac culminating in the sign Capricorn, and abstract when regarded from the *spiral* nature of the zodiac

Time and Space

represented by the sign Aquarius. From Aries to Scorpio, or from the brain to the organs of generation Mars has chief rule, and *for the majority of mankind at the present period Mars is the ruling planet of the human family:* but after the series of great wars we have now entered upon is over, it will have less power than formerly. As already explained in the previous course of lectures, Mars governs the senses in the majority of cases and binds men to their sense perceptions only.

The signs Capricorn and Aquarius govern those parts of the body that have nothing to do with generation, the knees and the ankles, the two centres from which the whole body is bent, either for the purposes of kneeling or walking. Saturn governs these two signs exclusively, and, corresponding with the signs just mentioned, governs the bony structure, or that which supports the whole body. Rigidity and flexibility are both seen to be governed by Saturn; the ability to stand upright or to bend. Standing and walking, in the very widest sense, as well as kneeling are therefore primarily due to the subtle influence of Saturn. This gives us a key to Saturn's influence upon character, for kneeling is a sign of humility, reverence, and submission, and is quite opposed to the martian spirit of assertion and forcefulness. The movement of the joints in walking is also a characteristic of Saturn, whose influence on

Rigidity, and Flexibility

character is to walk and obey the law of motion, at the same time keeping rigid and upright.

In Natal Astrology Saturn particularly denotes that part of the Ego which is in manifestation, representing the Personality—the concrete half-animal half-human soul, whose immortality is conditional, depending upon the desires being polarised heavenward instead of earthward and upon the personal will being surrendered to the divine will, when the true humility which belongs to the sphere of Saturn recognises the will of the Father, as the supreme and all-embracing love which draws all men unto Him. The influence of Mars like a flame envelopes all four arms of the Cardinal Cross; and like the animal-man goes round in a circle to accomplish its ends. Saturn however raises the man to an erect and upright position through the bony structure, which is a frame-work that keeps the whole body erect, and in this position it is an emblem of the mind which keeps a man upright.

True Humility

Saturn's influence not only effectually separates mind from feeling that is wholly personal, but also sensation from emotion, and mind from mind. The mind of each individual has a higher and a lower tendency; the higher being more concerned with principles, abstractions and synthesis, and the lower with concrete thoughts, external perception and analysis. For this reason

Scaffolding

Saturn is considered in esoteric astrology as the "bridge" between the lower and the higher, the personality and the true individuality. Saturn is perhaps better understood as the Reaper, for it collects and retains the impressions made upon the consciousness through actual first-hand experience. It is essentially the planet of EXPERIENCE; for it gathers up the fruits of every experience and hands on all that is worth retaining to the individual soul. It is therefore very often termed the individualising planet, and it is said by those who study astrology deeply as occultists that Saturn represents the scaffolding around the real self while the edifice of the individuality is in the process of building. Hence also the importance of Saturn's influence when laying foundation stones, commencing building operations, and so on.

The Tester or Tempter

It is not possible to define all the reapings of Saturn, neither can we hope fully to understand the peculiar influences of Saturn, which are different from those planets inferior to him; for strange as it may sound, Saturn's influence is unique where the unfoldment of the spiritual nature is concerned. In the "Mysteries" the planetary angel connected with the planet Saturn tested and tried every vesture of the Soul, so that nought should mar its final beauty. We may however find many clues to the influence of Saturn by racing that influence over the many virtues it bestows upon those who identify themselves with this planet. For it has been associated with the destinies of man, warring against mankind in order to subdue the arrogant will of the lower man to the divine.

The higher morality of Saturn's influence over mankind begins with the KNOWLEDGE of good and evil, and this knowledge may be termed conscience, or the result of past experiences. The true morality of the influence of Mars arises out of devotion and purified love, but it is always a personal devotion, or love to another personality, rarely if ever abstract. Saturn's peculiar morality on the other hand is not the result of personal love to an embodied ideal so much as love of duty, and therefore a morality based on justice, responsibility, and what is eventually to become the germ of truth. The idea that the morality arising out of Saturn's influence leads a man to a realisation of the truth inclines us to think that Saturn may signify truth, and therefore as a virtue truth is probably the bridge between the lower and the higher mind. "The truth will set man free," is an occult saying; there is nothing that binds us more than the illusion that we are separate, and the truth that shall set man free is the knowledge of good and evil—or the truth that there is only *ONE* reality in, and through, and behind, all worlds.

Morality: Saturnian and Martian

In Egyptian symbolism Set is the same as the planet MARS, and the animal nature of man. Seb is the planet

Set—
Seb—
Thoth—

SATURN, the tester of the soul, and Thoth the planet MERCURY; and in all the conflicts over the soul it is Seb and Thoth who bring about the at-onement between the opposing forces. Seb or Saturn is a race builder, a builder of nations as well as of individuals. This is one of the secrets of Saturn; he is a builder of Universes, although he is concerned in the creation and dissolution of the small as well as the great.

The perfection of *science* is the province of Saturn, and through science the perfection of civilisation as well.

In Hindu astrology, of the three great aspects of the trinity, Saturn is related to the god Shiva more than to Vishnu or Jupiter. Saturn in this respect is the destroyer who dissolves only to build anew, and its influence therefore appears to act in a manner contrary to that of Jupiter, who is the nourisher and preserver of all forms.

Bramah,
Vishnu,
Shiva

We are now witnessing the Saturnian influence which is playing an important part in the destruction of our present artificial civilisation; for the real crime of Germany, as Mr. J. L. Garvin editor of the *Observer* pointed out in an address delivered recently before the National Liberal Club, "is the perversion of science and thought and civilised technique to the purpose of destruction. It is the

A Breaking Down,—
and then a Rebuilding

crime of turning civilisation against itself." For while Saturn may not be the *actual* Regenerator, this planet certainly seems to be the herald of the Great Intelligence who is known as the Regenerator; and in character building we always find a breaking down before a rebuilding, and a scientific study of the influence of Saturn in each of the Twelve Signs of the Zodiac as well as the influence of Saturn in each of the Twelve Houses of the Horoscope would reveal much of the methods of Saturn's influence in the way of preparation for a rebuilding of the vehicles of manifestation through a refining process.

A Retarding Force

It is also the influence which appears to cause friction between the physical, emotional and mental vehicles, and which seems to act as a retarding force, and so gives its stability to all bodies; and from the standpoint of its being a hardening influence it is in all probability the chief cause of permanent magnetism[8] in all solid or mineral matter. By carefully tracing this peculiarity through the various kingdoms we find that in the mineral world Saturn's influence is probably electro-magnetic; it seems to be responsible for all the vibrations in dense mineral matter, and from the polarity of the Moon with Saturn there arise the vibrations

[8] (This expression is not here used in the restricted and technical sense in which "permanent magnetism" is said to be induced in a piece of steel by certain processes.)

which stimulate all mineral and inorganic matter into attraction with matter of an opposite nature. This produces cohesion, or union and aggregation, and may partly account for the powers and virtues that astrologers have always attributed to gems and precious stones.

Physical Influence: Earthy Signs

Scientific astrology teaches that Saturn's influence over the mineral atoms is cohesive or binding. It produces centres of force by inducing a rotary motion in the fixed signs of the Zodiac, and in the sign Taurus (the sign of the "Bull" in Ezekiel's wheel) it gives the greatest *stability* as a physical or earthy sign. It stimulates the nerve force in the mutable signs, and in the sign Virgo, the most mutable of the earthy signs, by a vibratory motion it gives this earthy sign its physical flexibility and *responsiveness*. It awakens the *apperception* of the cardinal signs, and in the sign Capricorn gives translatory motion expressed as activity and changeability allied to a peculiar stability. The influence of Saturn over the earthy signs and physical matter is in fact decidedly electro-magnetic, mainly electric and vitalizing in the *planet*, magnetic and receptive in the *sign*; and each sign expresses this magnetic life in terms of its own nature,—in Taurus as magnetic healing, for example, in Virgo as astral or psychic sensitiveness, and in Capricorn as mental activity, etc.

We may also trace Saturn's influence over the earthy

or physical signs through the law of vibration as stated above, seeing the rotary motion in the sign Taurus, the vibratory mode in the sign Virgo and the translatory in the sign Capricorn.[4] The link between earth and water is an electro-magnetic one, linking the mineral with the vegetable world; so that the influence of Saturn represents the bridge between the two.

Over the watery signs, or the vegetable world, the influence of Saturn is vital-chemical and metabolic. It marks the beginning of a definite cell life and growth preparatory to *organisation.* Saturn as a dominant influence over the mineral kingdom now loses its intense rigidity and density, and joins with the fluidic lunar influence in the shaping of forms; this is the first sub-influence of Saturn when the involution of the elemental essence connected with Saturn into matter is complete; and while Saturn's influence underlies all physical matter within the vegetable kingdom, through the watery signs, it works as a refining influence with another sub-influence,—each planet attracting a sub-influence of the other planets. Joined with the Moon, Saturn has a vital-chemical influence over the whole of vegetation. Earthy and watery signs have an affinity through an aspect or geometrical relationship that is harmonious, known as the sextile aspect of 60°, and from

Physical Influence: Watery Signs

[4] See *How to Judge a Nativity*, Chapter II.

the simplest lichen to the gigantic oak tree this influence is at work, shaping forms and giving *stability* and endurance.

The evolutionary process is a gradual preparation and refinement of matter under the influence of Saturn, which is the link between the many and various departments of Nature; and with each refinement there comes a higher vibratory activity. It is the *cold* influence of Saturn which causes the electro-magnetism to affect the whole of physical matter, probably through chemical decomposition producing positive and negative aspects out of which a middle influence, or birth of a new form of life, takes place; that middle factor *is really the essence of the influence itself*, which takes the form of a repellent or attractive magnetism in the mineral world, and a vital-chemical action in the vegetable world.

Physical Influence: Fiery Signs

In the animal kingdom, governed by the fiery signs of the zodiac, the life element itself is brought to its greatest point of activity. It is said that Nature abhors a vacuum, and there is no gap between the vegetable and the animal worlds; for just as the offspring of the electro-magnetic energy produces chemical compounds, so is the vibratory action between the vegetable and animal worlds raised to the point where the highly evolved vegetable cell is ready to receive the warmth of the animal life impulse from the Martian sphere, which vitalises all things in terms of sensation and muscular energy. Nutrition and reproduction under the mighty influence of Jupiter the nourisher are inherent in every cell, each cell through the slow and steady refining influence of Saturn being prepared for the manifestation of the new life-cycle which follows from the mineral upwards on into the human in orderly succession. In the animal world the positive forces have charged the life of the animal with reproductive energy, and the cells have become highly organised and complex, and the union of animals is now the result of powerful generative forces under the passional element of Mars. At a certain period of the earth's evolution Animal Man took possession of the earth, and then a new order of evolution began. Animal bodies had been prepared by the slow process of Nature under the preparatory or organising influence of Saturn, and then from the individualising influence of Saturn the soul of the animal was born, and as an individual soul it has a separate existence apart from the group soul.[5] The life element in the sign Leo has the germs of all Lions-to-be, and we have not to travel very far with our scientific imagination to learn how clearly the whole of the physical organism is typified by the signs of the zodiacs.

The magnetism and the lines of crystallisation in solid mineral matter are ruled by Saturn; the axes of growth

---

[5] For further particulars regarding the Group Soul, see *A Study in Consciousness*, Chap. V.

in the vegetable also are ruled by him, and the bony structure of the animal. What then does Saturn give to the human creature in addition, since it has held rule all along from the mineral through the vegetable to the highly organised animal frame?

The mystery connected with the influence of Saturn is one that cannot easily be stated because it is so apt to cause confusion in the minds of those who do not think astrologically. But whatever types of forms are latent in the subjective world, such as the "prototypes" of the lunar zodiac and of our ethero-physical ancestors, Saturn makes dense, and thus *materialises* that model or type; and it does more, for it plays the part of the destroyer of all forms that under its influence have hardened TOO MUCH. In this sense we can understand why Saturn's influence produces chronic ailments, the opposite to those that are acute, and therefore destroys life by decay and wasting diseases.

The Mystery of Saturn

The first mystery of Saturn lies in the combination of a series of influences forming a perfect or ideal trinity which is rooted in the Supreme Intelligence who is the One life-giver to all forms. This trinity is astrologically represented by the three planets Saturn, Jupiter, and Mars. Saturn governs the mineral, or physical world, as we have seen, and while hardening and binding all forms *until they have served their purpose in the evolutionary process*, he is also the dissolver of all forms.

That which survives the destruction of the form is the soul or inner essence of it, which gains a temporary or individual recognition of itself and is therefore the starting point of the "I," self-identity or the individual ego. In a very definite sense the mystery of Saturn was declared by the ancient astrologers when they affirmed that lead, the metal of Saturn, was a much nobler substance than gold.[6] They said "It is the living earth in which the soul of gold is joined to Mercury that they may bring forth Adam and his wife, Eve. Wherefore since the highest has so lowered itself as to become the lowest, we may expect that its blood may be the means of redeeming all its brethren."

The Christ in His great love and wisdom interpreted this idea: "He who is greatest amongst you let him be your servant."

Saturn's influence alone however would bind forever were it not subject to limitation, and were it not itself *the planet of time or limitation.* Jupiter's influence is preserving and expanding, and it becomes potent as an organising influence in the subtler realms, when Saturn has refined every atom to its appropriate dimensions for working in the field for which it has been prepared. Saturn is therefore, as already stated, the builder and Jupiter the preserver of that which has been built.

---

[6] *Cf Merchant of Venice,* iii 2. Portia says: "I am locked in one of them; if you do love me, you will find me out. . . ." Bassanio chooses the *leaden* casket, and finds therein her portrait.

The influence of Mars is that of the energizer or mover, giving activity or motion to that which Saturn has built and Jupiter has preserved. In this broad sense Saturn may be said to be lord over humanity in the physical world, or all concrete forms such as the personality of man which is subject to *time.* It is by the refining of the animal nature, under the frictional influence of Saturn, that the human has birth; in other words, the vibrations of Saturn are more enduring than Mars, the latter as already said projecting all force outward and the former turning it inward.

It is in the human form that the great struggle between the animal life and the spiritual unfoldment takes place. In the first stage the influence of Saturn is in subjection to that of Mars. In the second stage, Saturn and Mars are in conflict; and in the third and final stage Saturn's influence triumphs over Mars.[7] Mars represents the impulse of the senses and Saturn the "I" or the individualizing life forces seeking *self*-consciousness. We may trace the whole of the perfecting of the FORM side of manifestation by Saturn's influence in the negative signs from Cancer to Capricorn, ruled (or rather over-ruled) by the Moon, where Saturn denotes the feminine side of humanity; and by the combinations or polarities or affinities of these negative signs we can trace the growth of instinct through sensation and feeling to

---

[7] Observe that Shakespeare's drama of the "Taming of the Shrew" follows this same course.

intuition and perfect receptivity, a steady and gradual refinement and increase of vibratory power until the whole of the body is sufficiently pure and moral to become a medium or channel for the higher spiritual life.

The limit of the FORM itself, so far as the required size and structure are concerned, had been reached under the limiting influence of Saturn when man took possession of his animal physical body. But the expansion of the LIFE on the positive side from Leo to Aquarius has not yet reached the limiting stage at which intellect, or mind, can go no farther. The process of the changing *form*, under Saturn's influence, is going on subjectively within man through his feminine nature; and the process of the changing *life* proceeds through his internal life, as expressed by the positive or masculine signs. This takes place through the same laws of nutrition and reproduction until man has ceased growing and feeling and thinking in his physical body only. He grows and feels and thinks through evolving his opposite; that is, by seeking and finding his own polarity or affinity; and in the process he refines both life and form, and rises in consciousness until complete self-consciousness is reached. From the physical standpoint all life and form are seeking equilibrium, as typified by the exaltation of the planet Saturn in the sign Libra, the

Limit not yet Reached

sign of the perfectly balanced form. Indeed Libra is said to be the commencement of the zodiac for the human man just as Aries is for the animal man. But before we leave the physical aspect of Saturn for the psychic or soul aspect, let us consider the influence of Saturn in relation to the birth of a human being.

Before man came to inhabit this planet the physical conditions had been prepared for him. He himself had elsewhere evolved to the condition of a soul, and the earth was then at that stage of its evolution at which the mineral kingdom only had reached perfection. The story of man's evolution in the past is long and complicated.

Whence came Man?

In Mrs Besant's *Pedigree of Man* a very clear definition of man is given (p. 22):—"'Man' is that being in the universe, *in whatever part of the universe he may be and whatever form he may have,* in whom highest Spirit and lowest Matter are joined together by Intelligence, thus ultimately making a manifested God, who will then go forth conquering and to conquer, through the illimitable future that stretches before him": (italics ours). This definition will well repay thought.

A Definition of "MAN"

Astrologically speaking, there are many "*I*'s" in us until we reach the great and relatively permanent "*I*" of Saturn; but each stage of our progress is marked by a Saturnian sub-influence, producing stages of affinity or polarity and opposition. We are (our consciousness is) dual, recognising subject and object, from the densest forms of matter to the most refined state of intelligence, progressing in definiteness and subtlety and refinement until we reach a state of complete isolation and full self-consciousness and know ourselves as individuals, distinct and apart from all other selves; and then we finally arrive at the middle stage, zodiacally symbolised by the humane sign Libra, of "balance" between the self and the not-self, the real and the unreal, the true and the seeming, the darkness and the light, Death and Immortality.

THE BRIDGE

In this sense Saturn is the great Bridge through many personalities, the bridge of self-consciousness *leading* first from simple consciousness to self-consciousness, and then from self-consciousness to the threshold of super, or cosmic, consciousness. In the former stage we are building the *individual ego*, while in the later stage the individual ego is merged or expanded into the spiritual self; but the human personality is always the bridge between matter or the animal, and spirit. The whole field of Saturn's influence over man in this human evolution is one of struggle, a struggle for the survival of the fittest, and we may trace this struggle astrologically from the beginning of the lunar influence in the fleeting, vague and shadowy forms, to the Saturnian 'focussing' influence of clearness and definiteness and refinement, with considerable advantage to our own moral growth and spiritual unfoldment.

The Permanent Atom

Commencing with the physical birth of a child, we find the Moon and Saturn working in complete accord with one another, the Moon always 'shaping' the form which Saturn 'hardens' within certain well-defined limits. Before conception takes place the etheric mould, or pattern, upon which the physical body is to be built, is first in the womb. This etheric or lunar body is laid down by the agents of the great Lords of Karma at a time that will decide the moment of physical birth, and this is the moment of the so-called Pre-natal Epoch; an epoch that none but an occultist or an esoteric astrologer can fully understand. Then comes the germ bearing the physical permanent atom,[8] with the vital electro-magnetic power that is to fructify it. The Moon's place at the pre-natal epoch decides the ascending degree of the rising sign at birth and thence the meridian and other angles. The relation of the father of the child to the planet Saturn decides the hereditary traits, habits and general *physical* conditions of the child; and the moment of conception is the time

---

[8] For a full account of the Permanent Atom see Mrs. Besant's *Study in Consciousness*, Ch. iv.

when the permanent atom, transmitted by the father, has successfully joined the etheric mould in the womb of the mother.

Although the planetary influences contribute something to the birth of a child, the polarity of the Moon and Saturn decides the nature of the child to be born. The Moon is connected with the shadowy lunar, or etheric body; Jupiter with the ovum and the preserving influence; Saturn with the permanent physical atom, and Mars with the male cell or spermatozoon and with the desire element. Again, Saturn signifies the nature of the soul about to be reborn; Jupiter, the living matter that will form its body; and Mars the desire or longing for life that brings it to incarnation.

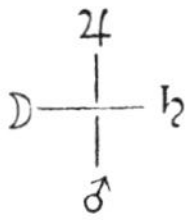

Here we have an interesting and instructive clue to the influence of Saturn over all permanent physical conditions. From the first functioning of the permanent physical atom to the end of the cycle, the mighty influence of Saturn holds sway until perfection is secured or the Christ spirit made manifest in the flesh. The occult teaching on this subject is very explicit and may be given for the helping of the many genuine students of astrology studying to help the world. "The physical body is shaped after the model created by the lords of Karma. . . . one of the Kama Devas guides the

From Savage to Christ . . .

physical atom by the agency of . . . to the body of the father chosen as suitable by past ties, and as able by nation, by family, by type, by hereditary peculiarities, to provide from his own body some of the materials needed. . . . Moreover the etheric double, after which the dense body is built, particle by particle, has for its nucleus the permanent atom. The permanent atom is carried by one of the spermatozoa into the womb of the mother, and therein, on fertilization, enters into an ovum. Its presence (*i.e.* the permanent atom) is not absolutely necessary to conception, and the stages that follow thereon may manifest themselves without it, but no 'quickening' can occur unless a permanent atom is within the fœtal form."

Living Pearls

It is important to note that this permanent atom, which comes from the father, is the nucleus around which the etheric double is built. The dense body is formed almost entirely of materials supplied by the mother. Astrological students owe a great debt of gratitude to Modern Theosophy and its leading exponents—a debt that will take much to repay—for the lucid and instructive information that has been given with regard to the Permanent Atoms, which are the living "pearls" strung upon the chord of life. Indeed, the particulars thus made known regarding the permanent atom, which we have after careful study traced to the influence of the planetary sphere of Saturn, will do much to bring

Astrology into scientific relations with the study of embryology.

H. P. Blavatsky cites the embryologist-philosopher Weissmann in support of this, for he "shows one infinitesimal cell, out of millions of others at work in the formation of an organism, alone and unaided determining, by means of constant segmentation and multiplication, the correct image of the future man, or animal, in its physical, mental, and psychic characteristics. . . "Complete the physical plasm, mentioned above, the 'germinal cell' of man with all its material potentialities, with the 'spiritual plasm' so to say, or the fluid that contains the five lower principles of the six-principled Dhyânî—and you have the secret, if you are spiritual enough to understand it"; (*S.D.* i. 243).

Weissmann's Germ-Cell

Commenting upon this, Mrs. Besant says:—"A little study of physical heredity in the light of Weissmann's teachings will be sufficient to convince the student of the possibility of such a body as the permanent atom. A man reproduces the features of a long-past ancestor, shows out a physical peculiarity that characterised a forbear several centuries ago. We can trace the Stuart nose through a long series of portraits, and innumerable cases of such resemblances can be found. Why then should there be anything extraordinary in the idea that an atom should gather within itself not biophors, as

Potentialities of Vibration

in the germinal cell, but tendencies to repeat innumerable vibrations already practised. No spatial difficulty arises, any more than in the case of a string, from which numerous notes can be drawn by bowing it at different points, each note containing numerous overtones. We must not think of the minute space of an atom as crowded with innumerable vibrating bodies, but of a limited number of bodies, each capable of setting up innumerable vibrations."

If we meditate upon the possibilities of the permanent physical atom which, as a nucleus, we may now for all practical purposes associate with Saturn, we shall, by relating it to the signs of the zodiac, discover that it has two active and distinct modes of vibration, and one latent. Metaphorically speaking, as 'activity' it is connected with CAPRICORN, and as 'will' with AQUARIUS; but in PISCES it is comparatively speaking a *dumb note.*

SATURN as REAPER

Tracing the Karma or fate of Saturn from the past to the present and onward into the future, we shall be able to see upon what plane Saturn as the Reaper will act. In any Cardinal Sign, or in the angles, we may expect the major portion of fate to fall upon the physical plane through action, which action will be more fatalistic or pronounced in the tenth house, affecting honour, avocation and worldly reputation. It will, also, disturb the physical body through the house and sign it is in at birth, or at the pre-natal epoch. In a Fixed Sign or in a succedent house it will affect the will or the desires, thwarting or assisting according to its strength or weakness, and affecting the vital organ or the body governed by the fixed sign that Saturn is in at birth.

Stability, Activity, Adaptability

By careful study we may trace the sowing and the reaping in every horoscope, by combining the influence of Mars and Saturn in sign or house, and by relating them to the teachings that have been given on the laws of Karma. In this aspect of astrology Saturn represents "dharma," or duty,—though the word duty does not fully express all that is signified by dharma,—and it always indicates the high water mark of the Personal Ego and its relation to the individuality. Saturn in a Fixed Sign shows the stability of the ego, its power of resisting from without; in a Cardinal Sign its power to change and become immersed in activity; and in a Mutable Sign its powers of adaptability,—or, its liability to indecision, according to general tone of the nativity. An active student will now see the value of all those remarkable combinations carefully worked out in the astrological text book *The Art of Synthesis*, ch. xvii., xviii., and if these are related to Saturn we may at once know the kind of Ego we are dealing with when seeking to call out the responsiveness shown in the horoscope.

There are twelve major combinations arising out of the quadruplicities, and when these are related to each house we have a revelation that can be obtained from no other planet as far as character and destiny are concerned; for it is the clue to temperament and the attitude of mind of the personal ego for the time in incarnation. In Hebrew Astrology Saturn symbolises the generative organs, or the creative power thrown downwards into matter, and is therefore the Lord over Nature, the representative of all natural laws, or Justice. The evil or malefic nature of Saturn is therefore the *abuse* of Nature's laws, and the dark side of Nature is said to be ruled by the great God Pan—Saturn in its retributive or corrective aspect.

Twelve Combinations

If inference or intuition has not led to the discovery of the secret of Saturn from what has been said in the foregoing analysis of the influence of Saturn we may state it as the Sages of Old have told us:—"The tomb in which our King is buried, is that which we will call Saturn, and it is the key of the work of transmutation; happy is he who can salute this planet by its right name. It is a boon which is obtained by the blessing of God alone; it is not of him that willeth or him that runneth, but God bestoweth it upon whom he will."

"Thy plainness moves me more than eloquence, And here choose I"

The best types of the material Saturnian development

are symbolized by the sign Capricorn, the Goat, in the following description given for those born when the Sun is in that sign from December 21st to January 20th.

Capricorn, the Goat

"Those born during this period are indefatigable workers and able organisers. They shirk no duty, eagerly shoulder responsibility, which they discharge with despatch and in an eminently practical and common-sense manner. They are economical and intolerant of wastage both of time and money, and never commit to to-morrow that which can be done to-day. They are invariably punctual, both as to time and promise, and are forced into activity by a calm, quiet and deep-seated ambition. They give value for money and likewise demand it, and their mind is subtle, tactful and diplomatic."

The better types of the mental and spiritual types are symbolised by the sign Aquarius, the Water bearer—the highest being that bearer of 'living water' of which whoso drinketh shall not thirst again. The following description well summarises the general characteristics of this sign:—" One of the outstanding features of those born during the two above dates is their lack of snobbery, and as *caste*[9] to them is senseless, they estimate a man's value by his character and not by any of his

Aquarius, the Water Bearer

[9] (In the Western application of the term only, not in its original meaning.)

trappings. They are usually refined, and have a liking for art in some form or another ; but their favourite study is perhaps that of human nature itself, which they stand aside from, and watch intently. Although faithful as friends, their circle of such is limited, though they may have a crowd of acquaintances. Undemonstrative in affection (except to the few), they may be falsely judged as cold and unsympathetic. In youth they find it difficult to determine their avocation, as they are intolerant of restraint and dislike settling into a groove out of which it will be difficult to extricate themselves."

Illustrations

From the physical standpoint we may discover three distinct types of the Saturnian, two being shown in *The Art of Synthesis*, p. vii. No. 1, shows the studious brow and the thoughtful face giving the impression of a man who reflects upon what he observes, and who is given to contemplation upon all he has learned, seeking to link his knowledge with unseen causes. This is the scientific and philosophical type who is refined and clean in his life as well as his thoughts and feelings. No. 2, shows a more alert type, a man of acute and accurate perceptions, more fitted for business pursuits and commercial enterprises than for the part of scientist or philosopher. He looks an honest and straightforward man who is deliberate, cautious, patient, and reliable, having a good sense of responsibility and capable of handling men in his employ. His brow slopes backward, his nose is wry and his mouth firm and he has the appearance of a man who is decisive, conscientious and self-reliant. He is a good specimen of the medium or middle type of Saturnian, while a heavier and less alert type might be found in the ordinary road-mender or building-contractor's navvy, a man who is slow, ponderous, and not in any sense brilliant or alert, who moves and thinks slowly, has strong physical leanings and is more material and doubtful than the other types. This last represents the average Saturnian who is not aroused to any clear sense of his possibilities. He broods and may at times wonder but rarely puts himself out more than he can help, and is in fact a good specimen of indifference, lethargy and inertness. It will however be noticed that he is honest, plodding, and if laborious and obstinate he is at all events stolid and substantial. His day will come, and he will pass into No. 2 type and finally into No. 1; for it is the law of evolution that types shall pass from gross to fine, from density to refinement.

"Saturn is often depicted as a carrier of burdens, and astrologers find that it is the Saturnian upon whom the burden of sorrow falls; indeed many can trace their first taste of sorrow to an affliction of Saturn.

"In the early stages of evolution there is irresponsibility. The life of the savage, whose one idea becomes self-preservation, is an irresponsible one, and it is not until civilisation really begins that the awakening takes place, when the higher faculties are called into active use, and humanity passes from the stage of Mars to that of Saturn, from reckless impulse and careless indifference to steadiness, patience and concentration. There are many grades of Saturnian vibrations, each more or less binding. Saturn is the great lord of fate and time, and his decree is absolute, for not until the last fraction is paid will he loosen the bonds that have made what the Hindu astrologer calls Karma. . . ."

Rays of Truth, p. 83.

"YOGA.—The practice of meditation as a means of leading to spiritual liberation. Psycho-spiritual powers are obtained thereby, and induced ecstatic states lead to the clear and correct perception of the eternal truths, in both the visible and invisible universe."

H. P. BLAVATSKY, *Th. Glossary*, p. 381.

LECTURE II.

SYNOPSIS.—Saturn and Yoga—its relation to colour and the interlaced triangles—a Hindu story of a King, his Chief Counsellor and a charming Princess, illustrating the influence of Saturn—the influence of Saturn in the Twelve Signs of the Zodiac.

The Seven Steps of Saturn to the Throne of the Sun

(1) Take your life as you find it; do your duty well. (2) Do all things without personal attachment. (3) Destroy the evil in your own heart first, which will kill the evil around you, for a white surface will reflect a white light only. (4) Be good; be clean of thought and clean of heart. (5) The ceasing of sorrow is the aim of life. (6) Be gods and God will be yours. (7) You are He and He is you.

Concentration, Meditation, Contemplation

In the last lecture we said that a clue might be found to the influence of Saturn by tracing the virtues that have been attributed by astrologers to that planet. We know by experience that these virtues are almost the reverse of those of the impulsive Mars, and the first touch of Saturn's influence is realised in restraint or repression—in one word, *limitation.* The most noticeable quality of Saturn's influence is the virtue of self-control, and until a man is fully self-controlled he has still some of the impulsiveness of the animal nature struggling for mastery. This places Saturn's influence decidedly on the side of the human as against the animal. From self-control three steps lead to liberation or freedom from the bondage of the lower nature, and they are: CONCENTRATION, MEDITATION, and CONTEMPLATION.

These stages cannot be successfully accomplished without using some of the influence of Saturn. Mars is

Concentration

not a planet whose influence favours concentration, unless it be on *desire*, through feeling or emotion; and even then it is not of long duration, being easily affected by a change of desire or feeling. Concentration has been described as, "the hindering of the modifications of the thinking principle." If for the moment we consider the Mind in its pure or creative state as represented by the planet Venus, and the Lower Mind or that part of the mind that is expressed through the brain as under the influence of the Moon, Saturn is the bridge between the two which influences the concentration and steadies, for the time, the active mind. For instance, that which is termed the lower or personal mind is diffusive and changeable like the Moon, wandering from one object or idea to another; it is the influence of

Saturn, the planet whose pole is opposite to the Moon, which makes it one-pointed or able to hold one thought alone to the exclusion of all others, and so it is truly said that the mind is modified by every object that comes before it. The brain is the *instrument* of the mind and not the mind itself, as may be experienced by those who know how to stop the mind or make it active at will. This suggests the idea that Saturn is also closely allied to the WILL aspect of consciousness and that it acts as the immediate influence or agent of the will. Reason, however, leads to dispassion or the higher indifference which is not an aspect of will, but is more allied to the Justice side of Saturn's influence; so that we may safely say that the influence of Saturn is an aid to actual concentration. This will also apply to Saturn's influence on meditation as a whole, where the thoughts are brought to a focus; but the nature of any particular form of meditation can only be seen from the whole horoscope.

Meditation

In true and earnest meditation there is first a discrimination between the real and unreal, which seems to be a peculiarly saturnian quality. In its destructive or dissolving element the influence of Saturn from this standpoint transmutes the animal nature or those personal desires which are derived from the tendencies of Mars, through a process of discriminative analysis, rejecting the evil or the false and storing the fruit of all good or true thought, as well as feeling, and probably action; and this true discrimination between the real and the unreal leads to meditation.

There is another virtue which we attribute to Saturn, that of FORBEARANCE, which in the Yoga Aphorisms is said to consist in "not killing, veracity, not stealing, continence and not coveting." The truly Saturnian man will go to extremes in not killing or taking life which he cannot give, and for this reason he is more often than not a non-flesh-eater owing to the forbearance he has with regard to the slaughter and killing of animals for his food; he is also a truthful man, preferring truth to falsehood. He is usually far too honest to steal and would rather die of poverty than rob or steal from others. He is by preference a lover of continence owing to the strong tendencies to purity and perfect cleanliness which he rejoices in, and also, probably, from some natural instinct born in him. The dispassion which a true saturnian man possesses does not allow him to covet or seek to hold possessions. All the virtues of the Saturnian influence appear to be "cold" and "unattractive" to the Martian temperament, and this shows the tendency to abstract, or to discriminate and *separate* the real from the unreal, the true from the false.

Forbearance

This suggests that the influence of Saturn is peculiarly favourable to the ascetic, and may lead to the stage of

Yoga

the Sanyasi, or the Man who has purified his vehicles. The chief characteristic of Saturn is innate purity, and in its opposite nature to Mars we find the senses restrained through the purifying tendencies of Saturn. The first requisite in yoga is physical purity, for without the purification of the vehicles there can be no successful yoga. Yoga is of two classes, and is singularly saturnian in this respect. For there is Hatha Yoga, which (the true hatha yoga) corresponds to the earthy or Capricorn element of Saturn, and is concerned wholly with the vehicles or the form side of development; and there is Raja Yoga, or union with God through the consciousness, which corresponds to the airy or Aquarian element of Saturn.

If we are to understand the real nature of Saturn's influence we must look for it as governing the apex of a triangle that has for its base the signs Capricorn and Aquarius, the positive and negative houses of the plane Saturn. The apex of this triangle represented by the planet Saturn is the medium or link between the mind that is mixed with sensation, desire and personal selfishness, and the mind that is pure and unadulterated, free from worldly desires and attachments. We may think of Saturn's influence apart from the zodiac as the pure part of a Ray coming from the spiritual realms into the physical, and there becoming

♄
♑ ♒

adulterated by mixing with impure thoughts and feelings, which lead to personal or selfish actions. This pure part of the ray may be considered as the very highest notion of the "*I*" a human being can attain to whilst still remaining human. It is not the real or permanent "I," but the personal self in its highest phase when ready to merge or expand into the real spiritual self; and it has therefore the clearest sense of separateness that any part of the nature can have. Its very nature is separative, distinct and self-contained, and only loses that idea of self at the two poles of pure spiritual substance and dense matter. In pure substance it finds itself one with all other selves, and in dense matter it is lost in a multiplicity of other selves,—lost in a crowd as it were—so as to forget its own self, and yet not be consciously one with the other selves.

Three Stages of Saturn's Influence

If the idea is not made too concrete we may trace Saturn's influence in three definite stages starting from Saturn as an abstract influence at the point or apex of a triangle that has its base in the two signs Aquarius and Capricorn. At the apex, this influence of Saturn in the abstract may be thought of as related to Space and Extension, but at the base as related to Time and Limitation. THE FIRST STAGE of Saturn's influence is abstract at the apex, at the second stage of the Saturnian ray it is at the Aquarian side of the Saturnian triangle, and the third stage is at the Capricorn angle, as figured in the accompanying diagram.

We may treat of Saturn's influence Geometrically, or scientifically; in Colour Language, or philosophically; and in Sound, or metaphysically. Geometrically the rays of Saturn's pure or abstract influence end at the base of the triangle, and it becomes interwoven with those signs below the base of the triangle as a compound. The Ray of Saturn, itself, apart from the signs, is always a PURE Green, and is then when blended with the sign

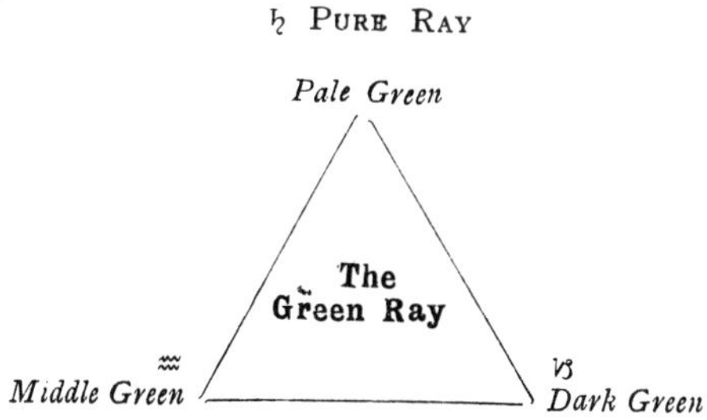

Capricorn or Aquarius (speaking only from the colour standpoint of course), a secondary colour, composed of the lighter and darker shades of green, and is as it were midway between the two primaries, Blue and Yellow (represented by Venus and Mercury). And in fact in the solar spectrum green, the colour of Saturn, is actually situated between blue and yellow, and fades into these on either side. When combined with the signs Aquarius and Capricorn it is a mixture, *not* a compound.

The Two Crosses

Saturn's relation to the cross, or the square aspect, (whether zodiacal or mundane) is conflicting. From the sign Aquarius we have a FIXED CROSS, square, or cube, by taking a straight line from the sign Aquarius to the sign Leo with a crosspiece to Taurus and Scorpio; and from the sign Capricorn a CARDINAL CROSS taking a straight line to the sign Cancer with a crosspiece to Aries and Libra. This we may illustrate by a diagram.

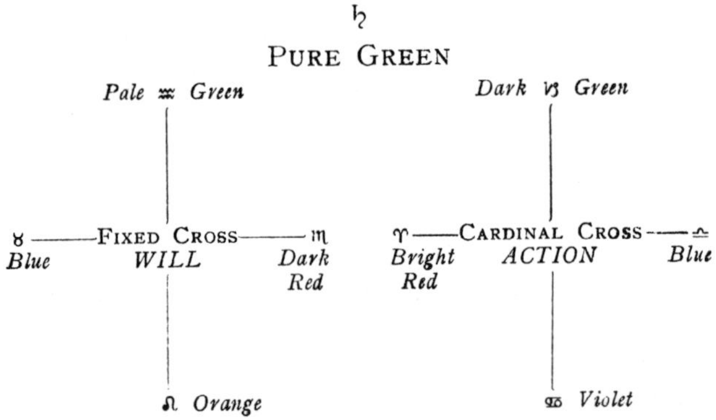

In the Fixed Cross the pale green ray of Aquarius is *compounded* in the signs Taurus, Leo and Scorpio; and in the Cardinal Cross the dark green ray of Capricorn is *compounded* in the signs Aries, Cancer and Libra. It would take too long to go into all the details of this compounding of the influence of Saturn through the signs above mentioned, but the intuitive student who has made any study of Esoteric Astrology will picture the relationship between Saturn's influence and what is known as the Lower Quarternary. For further enlightenment on the subject the student is recommended to study the twelve houses of the horoscope in Chapter XV of *Practical Astrology*, where it is shown that in the earthy signs Saturn harmonises Honour and Profession (♑) with Thought and Worldly Possessions (♉), and Service (♍); illustration C describing how the airy triplicity is worked out in the lower and higher self.

The Middle Ray

Students who are anxious to work out the relationship of the Saturnian or green ray to the others should note that green is the middle ray between the two extremes at the end of the spectrum, red and violet. Saturn is in its detriment in the sign Cancer and in its fall in the sign Aries—signs representing the violet and red rays respectively. Saturn is exalted in the sign Libra representing the indigo ray, and is neither strong nor weak but indifferent in the yellow and blue rays represented by the Mutable Cross.

A Hindu Story

Some Eastern Astrologers have an interesting method of describing the influence of the planets in an abstract sense, and there is a very charming story told by them of a KING, representing the Lord over the Personality whose name is synonymous with that of Saturn; a PRINCESS, whose name corresponds to Venus, and the King's CHIEF COUNSELLOR or adviser, whose name and that of the planet Mercury are the same.

The King, who was ruler over a vast territory, meaning the personal self with all its ramifications, was a misogynist, and his ministers were greatly troubled by the lack of an heir. So they caused all the most beautiful women they could find to be placed in the King's way so as to be seen by him on frequent occasions, by chance meetings or otherwise, in the hope of engaging his affections. But he hated women so much, that he even went so far as to threaten that he would have any woman killed who came in his path; his ministers, therefore, fearing the destruction of all the womenfolk in the nation, had to reverse their policy and keep every woman out of his sight. And in consequence of the utter failure of their plans they were in great despair.

One day a celebrated Painter came from a distant country and learned of the nation's distress. He was greatly concerned, but said he thought he could cure the King of his distrust and hatred, and asked to be admitted into his presence, as he desired to show him his pictures. The ministers gained the consent of the King, for the Painter's fame was world-wide, but the stipulation was made that *no woman's* picture should appear amongst the collection. In due course the Painter was admitted, with a warning that his life would be forfeited if the picture of a woman was found amongst his paintings. The King turned over the artist's paintings, admiring one after the other, until suddenly he came upon the portrait of a beautiful woman. Immediately he fell to the ground in a swoon, and while the ministers rushed to his assistance, the Painter fled into another room. After being roused from his faint, the King commanded that the Painter be brought before him. The ministers, however, fearing for the Painter's life declared that he had fled. But the Painter on hearing the King's cry had come into the apartment, and to the surprise of the ministers the King eagerly enquired of him as to the name of the beautiful woman whose portrait he had seen, and where she dwelt; for he said there could be no other woman on earth to compare with her.

The Painter replied that the lady was a Princess, and dwelt in a distant land; that she was unapproachable; for although she had had many suitors, wealthy and distinguished, she had rejected all. Her method of receiving a suitor was a strange one. He was required to put questions or "riddles" to her, and only if he could succeed in propounding some riddle that she entirely failed to answer would she consent to receive his attentions: so far, all aspirants without exception had failed, for she had answered every question without difficulty. Nothing daunted, the King was anxious to make the attempt and was eager to set out at once, but the Painter said she lived at a great distance in a lonely castle, well guarded. The King replied that he would give him great wealth if he would reveal the name of the Princess and where she dwelt, but that if he refused he should instantly be put to death. The Painter having given the required information, the King was impatient to set off at once, without waiting for his retinue, so much was he in love with the face he had seen. His Chief Counsellor however urged him on no account to go without him, as he would be able to propound riddles that the Princess might not be able to answer.

The story continues with the journey and the meeting, and tells how the King every day fell deeper and deeper in love. The Princess would only see the King and his adviser at *sunset*, when the riddle was to be propounded, and so the King spent each day longing for the sunset hour when he could see her.

The story is a long one, for each of the one and twenty riddles is a story in itself. But the whole illustrates the idea that the PRINCESS represents the planet Venus, symbolising the human soul in its virgin purity; that the CHIEF COUNSELLOR is a representative of the planet Mercury, symbolising the Thinker; and that the KING is the planet Saturn, or the ray *between* the desires of the flesh and the purified mind.

This symbology is well illustrated by the connection of the houses of Saturn with those of Venus and

The Unanswerable Question

Mercury. VENUS is the Soul, and MERCURY the Thinker, but it is not until the King or the self represented by SATURN asked the Princess directly, that is without the intervention of his Chief Counsellor, a question to which she could not give a reply, that he was able to win her. He asked her to tell him herself what riddle he should ask in order that he might obtain her; and she could not answer, for she loved him.

☽—♄
☉—♄

It is in the setting sign Libra, ruled by Venus, that Saturn is exalted. The affliction of Venus by Saturn is the greatest cross the soul can bear, since the struggle between the two must sooner or later end in a victory for one or the other, with far-reaching results. Saturn on the Fixed or Cardinal cross modifies or accentuates its influence for good or evil. The stories concerning St. George and the Dragon are astrological myths conveying true ideas; for it is the Moon, giver of life to our globe, that has its first struggle with Saturn; and finally the Sun, giver of life to the whole solar system, who combats the Saturnian influence. Saturn is the great adversary who first contests with the personality and finally the individuality, and one or the other must win; and in the long run of many lives it is the Higher Self who wins. A metaphysical study of Saturn's influence will reveal the fact that Saturn is directly and decidedly connected with character building; and as such Saturn is the only real indicator of fate and destiny and also, what is far more important, is the only factor in the great problem of fate and free will.

Ezekiel's Wheel

From the standpoint of the Cross of the Lower Quarternary (indicated by the angular house of the horoscope) the personality represented by it is under the bane of fate up to the extent indicated by that sign of the cross in which Saturn is placed; and until that cross is lifted by the purification of the character of a man he is subject to his particular personal Karma. In Ezekiel, Chapter 1, this Cross is described by the prophet as follows: "And I looked, and, behold, a whirlwind came out of the north, a great cloud, and a fire infolding itself, and a brightness was about it, and out of the midst thereof as the colour of amber, out of the midst of the fire. Also out of the midst thereof came the likeness of four living creatures. And this was their appearance; they had the likeness of a man. And every one had four faces, and every one had four wings." He then proceeds to describe the wheels and the appearance of the faces, one had the face of an ox (Taurus), and one the face of a man (Aquarius); another had the face of a lion (Leo), and another the face of an eagle (Scorpio). This is an illustration of the great God Shiva who sits in the burning ground, and is translated astrologically into Saturn on the human cross in which the animal is transmuted through Aquarius, the sign of the MAN.

Fatalists, working towards Freedom

In our study of character and the influence of Saturn there is one word used in philosophy which seems completely to describe Saturn's influence upon character; it is, *determinism*. A true Saturnian man is practical, firm, decisive, definite, but slow to form resolutions. He usually determines his line of action or comes to a definite conclusion before he acts, but having once decided is slow to be moved from his purpose. It is just this peculiarity of Saturn's attitude which makes Saturnian men fatalists; for more often than not they decree their own fate by their decisions, and limit themselves by their premeditated desires or choice. This very attitude, however, makes for eventual freedom, since they are always testing the limitations and conquering them by higher and higher determinations and by patient labourings to succeed in the conquest of matter.

CHARACTER is DESTINY

From the standpoint of that important statement "CHARACTER IS DESTINY," it is quite possible to predict the major portion of a person's life by a careful study of the *sign* which the planet Saturn occupies at birth, considered together with its position and aspects. We say that Saturn is the planet of limitation because the nature of the sign, representing a peculiar type of matter, limits and restricts the powers of the individualised self represented by Saturn. In nine cases out of ten a man who knows anything definite about himself will readily identify himself with the characteristics of the sign occupied by Saturn at birth. Deep in the nature of every person having Saturn in a watery sign, we find strong and powerful emotions; in the fiery signs we find a strong mental tendency; and so on. It is the circle of the zodiac which constrains and decides the motives, bias or tendency of each planet's influence, and it is this tendency which appears to be so fatalistic—and which really *is* fatal while we are ignorant of its nature.

The first limitation for us all is the moment of our birth, when we come upon the stage of life, and circumstances and environment are as we find them. Astrologically speaking, these circumstances find their correspondence in the houses or mundane divisions of the horoscope. We are born with planets rising, culminating, setting, or having passed below the horizon; and we are conditioned accordingly. We are also born with the planets placed in certain zodiacal signs; and we partake of their nature, more or less. So that by a careful study of Natal Astrology we should be able to find out just where we are placed in the scale of human evolution. When we have controlled our impulses, and are no longer attracted or repelled too easily by agreeable

The First Limitation

or disagreeable persons and things in our environment, we may examine the stage at which we have arrived and try to understand the particular influence to which we *do* most readily respond. So far as the majority of students are concerned, it will be either a *Martian* or a *Saturnian* vibration which dominates; for these so-called 'malefic' influences are ruling the majority of human beings in the world to-day.

Motive

The influence of Mars as we have already seen is compelling and impulsive, and under its influence a man is guided more by feeling than by mind or reason; the mind and the feelings are very mixed, and the one rarely acts without the other. But the feelings of Mars (as shown in our previous Course of Lectures) may be purified to a very high degree, and then the motive for action becomes a moral one. It is the MOTIVE that counts in all our decisions, for motive is behind Will and Action. What then is the motive of the Saturnian man? It is of quite a different nature from that of Mars. When a Mars man is moral it is through his *love nature*, or his devotional feelings to the object of his adoration. But a Saturnian man is moral from a *sense of justice*, of right as against wrong, and he is moved more by his conscience than by his emotions.

It is one of the secrets of the successful synthesis of a nativity to be able to answer the question: What is the Chief Motive underlying the impulses, and the actions?

While it is not fair or strictly accurate to say that the Martian temperament is below that of the Saturnian, there are nevertheless cases where a Saturnian temperament will be prompted to good action by motives that would not appeal to the Martian. Great devotion will do more for a man of the Martian temperament than the calm and strict justice or will of the Saturnian, but the influence of Saturn is probably destined to carry a human being to far greater service and usefulness than the impulse of Mars can achieve. The Mars influence carried to a great height will make a man a hero, while Saturn's influence will produce the martyr. It is just a question of motive. The martyr suffers for a cause or a principle, and will suffer persecution unto death, and it is more often than not for the sake of the *truth* enshrined in a cause or principle that the sacrifice is made or the suffering undergone. Now the hero will also give his life, but it will be under stress of a great emotion or when moved to risk all for a purpose. The Hero is quick to act, the Martyr slow. In occult phraseology Mars seeks the way without, and Saturn seeks the way within. It is very curious to note the wide difference between the influence of Mars and that of Saturn; yet although they are the two

Martian and Saturnian Temperaments contrasted

extremes in nature, they may both produce the same result, only through different methods. A Mars man is physically courageous, and where expression and external strength are concerned he seems to score in an argument or an enterprise; but he is only courageous for the time and while feeling moves him. Saturn on the other hand appears to be fearful, timid and shy. It is a matter of temperament. The Saturnian influence causes a nervous tension and a tendency towards restraint and reserve which looks like fear; but after the first shock the Saturnian man will pull himself together and stand his ground quite fearlessly. This brings up a very interesting point in connection with Saturn where religion or ethics is concerned. Mars does not make a man religious in the strict sense of the word, but it will bring him to religion through the uplifting tendency of his emotional nature towards Devotion; and a martian man may therefore be saved by religious experiences.

Not so the Saturnian man. The text most appropriate to the Saturnian is that of the wise King who wrote "The fear of the Lord is the beginning of Wisdom" (*Prov.* ix, 10). But it is not a dread or apprehension, it is the fear mentioned in the first epistle of Peter, (ii, 17), "Fear God; Honour the King." Religion may follow for a Saturnian man when he has observed the moral law, and exhausted

Saturnian Religion

all the requirements of duty;[10] and although he may not have the physical courage of the Mars man he has a far deeper sense of his responsibilities. This is why the Saturnian is found with an inclination towards the Roman Catholic religion, and makes a good priest; for he loves counsels of perfection, confessing his sins, doing penance, etc.

In the book *Practical Astrology*, written over twenty years ago, a list was given of the tendencies of Saturn when active and passive, showing the many and varying moods expressed by Saturn's influence. These descriptions, if amplified by the nature of the sign occupied by Saturn, should be valuable to every student. We may therefore profitably study the nature of Saturn in each of the twelve zodiacal signs, first remembering that its sign- and house-position in every nativity is a *critical point* from which the whole horoscope is subdued, modified or accentuated. In fact it may in many cases be said to define the whole horoscope, since it tends to separate the finer influences of the nativity from the coarser.

Sign-Influence of Saturn

SATURN IN ARIES accentuates the active quality of the cardinal-fire sign Aries and stimulates to directive

---

10 "And the Young Man saith unto him, 'All these things have I kept from my youth up: what lack I yet?' . . . . sorrowful [*i.e.* serious]: for he had great possessions"; (Matthew xix, 20, 22).

♄ - ♈

action by the forming of plans, awakening the ambitious side of the nature, but inclining to impulsive actions. The tendency of this influence will be to organise schemes, and as it will give the ability to direct and control others it will bring success through the exercise of authority and by commanding obedience in others. This ability to see ahead should be useful, if the plans can be carried out by others less impulsive; and if the other tendencies in the horoscope harmonise, there should be capacity both to plan and to carry out the plan effectively through the exercise of forethought. The activity excited by this influence produces enough energy to carry through all responsibilities by prompt action. Mental activity and a determined spirit are denoted.

♄ - ♉

SATURN IN TAURUS brings into operation the stability aspect of the fixed-earth sign Taurus, and Saturn is usually well placed in this and denotes many possibilities, since the desire nature of the Will should be fixed and the individuality considerably strengthened, producing persistent effort and a persevering nature, although slow, rather laborious and painstaking. There will however be several drawbacks, such as too much reserve, pride, and a tendency to be doubting or sceptical, in a materialistic sense. On the other hand there would be a very reverential feeling and a tendency to respect authority and to be faithful where confidence was once given. It favours the practical side of the nature. There will be a latent tendency toward the occult, and a deep love of the mystical; in fact the spiritual side of the nature although very slow to unfold, would gradually be felt. This position gives a love of scents and perfumes; and the desire, although somewhat sensuous, should be toward depth and thoroughness. It best favours the vital temperament.

♄ - ♊

SATURN IN GEMINI will act through the harmonious aspect of the mutable-air sign Gemini. Saturn has not much affinity with the mutable signs in general, for it is more inclined to one-pointedness than to duality, and we might easily expect indecision or an inclination to sit on a fence where vital principles were concerned. It should however give leanings toward intellectual pursuits, with a tendency to follow two avocations at one time, or even a desire to be in two places at once; that is to say, the mind could easily be in one place while the body is in another. It should give liking for and attention to details, though not much concentration. Where the hands were employed as well as the mind it would be a favourable influence, and in this respect it should make good typists, shorthand clerks or book-keepers, secretaries, cashiers, etc. If the horoscope harmonises with this position, (that is to say, does not contradict by aspects, etc.), there would be a love of travel or of educational pursuits, and much versatility, together with rather subtle motives. Too much physical strain would bring nervous breakdown or affect the health, so that change of work or occupation would be desirable. Persons of the motive temperament would profit most by this position.

SATURN IN CANCER affects the emotionally active aspect of the cardinal-water sign Cancer and has much power over the emotional nature.

♄ - ♋

This is the sign in which Saturn is supposed to be very weak, and persons with this influence in the horoscope are not favoured by Saturnian persons or by those of the Saturnian temperament. These persons are certainly more or less under fate, and are often limited by circumstances and environment over which they have little or no control, although strange to say they have either a tenacious will or a very powerful desire nature. This influence is remarkable for the psychic tendencies it gives, and the intense love of the occult or mystical. It is, as might well be expected, a somewhat depressing influence owing to the extreme sensitiveness it produces both to things astral and physical. It favours the personal tendencies more than the individual, and it requires a very strong horoscope to support it, for unless this is the case it depletes the moral tendencies through a lack of any idea of the value of responsibility; but if the horoscope is a strong one it denotes much sympathy, a very receptive nature, and much responsiveness. In sickness or distress the virtues of this influence are readily seen, for it gives the power through responsiveness to feel all sorrow and suffering very keenly. To those who are too mediumistic it is fatal, but for those who are spiritually awakened it offers great possibilities. It favours the vital temperament, but is very inimical to the motive or mental.

SATURN IN LEO corresponds to the stability aspect of the fixed-fire sign Leo. It endows those under its influence with great mental vitality, a strong will and a strange temperament, in which mind, feeling and will are curiously mixed. If the love nature is not controlled it causes much prodigality. It tends to accentuate responsibilities, gives a keen sense of honour and much love of liberty or freedom. It makes the love nature conjugal, and often produces one great love in the life or a love for a few chosen friends. It favours abstract thinking, and everything of an enterprising or speculative nature; and while it tests faith, it gives inherent spirituality. It harmonises best with the vital temperament or the mental, but not with the motive.

♄ - ♌

SATURN IN VIRGO corresponds to the harmonious aspect of the mutable-earth sign Virgo. This is one of the very critical signs for Saturn, since motive counts for so much with those who are under this influence. To the

♄ - ♍

conventional or narrow types it is inimical, since it binds the Will or desire nature to physical considerations and inclines the mind to be too analytical, critical and unfortunately very often to fault-finding where it is quite unnecessary. It often produces much apprehension and dread of consequences and thus induces worry and anxiety, leading to nervous conditions. In the purer types, or those who are more broad minded, it inclines to science, to reason, and discrimination, and produces good literary critics, skilled proof-readers, journalists and chemists. There is an intermediate class of persons who are very self-introspective and somewhat psychic. This influence is of the conserving, retiring, and negative type. It inclines to depression, and a somewhat worm-like spirit of humility. It favours the chaste, the virtuous, and the truth seeker, and usually helps those of the motive temperament more than the vital; in the mental it produces unhappy and sceptical tendencies.

♄ - ♎

SATURN IN LIBRA corresponds to the activity aspect of the cardinal-air sign Libra. It is the sign in which Saturn is said to be exalted or to have its great power from the human standpoint. It denotes a well-balanced will or desire nature, and coincides with the influence of Saturn as the Bridge between the higher and lower half of the heavens, taken as the ascent or descent from the one to the other. It also coincides with the idea of Saturn as the planet of Justice, holding the sword in one hand and the scales in the other. It is a decidedly critical influence, since it places the Will or Desire nature in the balance between right and wrong, truth and falsehood. This influence depends *more than any other* (except perhaps Capricorn) on the whole trend of the nativity. It tends to bring the will to a state of evenness and to a condition where judgment is necessary to decide the choice of action. To the man of shallow intellect it is fatal, but to the man of judgment and intuition it means great things. It may be likened to a Soul in the scale of justice, being weighed throughout the whole of the current life, with great possibilities hanging upon the way the scales incline. It favours the artistic temperament.

♄ - ♏

SATURN IN SCORPIO corresponds to the fixed emotional aspect of the fixed-water sign Scorpio. This is a tragic influence, for the Will or Desire nature is rarely weak; but if it is weak then the life is one of tragedy and misfortune. It denotes powerful emotions, strong attachments and a very mystical or occult nature with enormous possibilities. It brings much fate into the life, mainly through the deaths of those to whom attachment is given, or through realisations connected with feeling. This is the best influence for regeneration or the transmutation of the emotional nature through suffering. Pain is the great teacher for all who have this influence strong at birth; and a very hard task is placed before those souls who have chosen it for their Karma. It gives the ability to probe secrets, to reason and analyse, and gives a great amount of innate shrewdness and penetration. It allows those under its influence to criticise and also to sit in judgment upon others; but where they love they can give abundantly, and where they hate they can hate successfully. They are never weak characters although they can be very wicked when the moral character is weak. They are decisive, very determined and possess some magical power of which they may or may not be aware. These are the real detectives, the watchers and the scrutinisers. Much depends upon the aspects Saturn forms from the sign and the house it is in for its perfect manifestation as a strong influence. It favours the occult, the mystical and the dramatic.

SATURN IN SAGITTARIUS corresponds to the harmonious aspect of the mutable-fire sign Sagittarius.

♄ - ♐

Saturn may be very strong or very weak in this sign. It favours the philosophical temperament more than the Will or Desire nature, and in some cases it gives a very frank, open and straightforward character. Its tendency is to separate the animal from the human; and here again we find Saturn acting as the bridge; and in this respect it sometimes weakens the will in this sign, but it may well be the personal and not the individual will. It favours persons of the religious type and also those of a scientific turn of mind. It also favours love of ceremony, ritual and the ordering of things on a plan, and therefore often gives great respect for law and order, religious ceremonies or symbolical representations. The desire nature is inspirational, reverential and aspiring. The duality of the sign is somewhat a drawback, but it favours two occupations or two different kinds of work. To the person born under a weak horoscope it denotes carelessness, indifference, rebellious tendencies and inclines to indecision, and many abuses. For this latter type "the fear of the Lord is the beginning of wisdom" surely.

♄ - ♑

SATURN IN CAPRICORN corresponds to the activity aspect of Saturn through the cardinal-air sign Capricorn. Saturn's influence should be strong in this sign, for it gives a love of power and mastery over others, but it is somewhat isolating and tends to loneliness and many limitations. It favours all who desire service, and it gives the Will to serve when the horoscope is harmonious. In this sign Saturn is the bridge between selfishness and service, either personally or individually. It is the sign in which Saturn may very easily accentuate the responsibilities by giving a strong sense of duty, for it makes the ideals practical. More depends upon the whole horoscope for this influence than when Saturn is placed in any other sign, even Libra.

SATURN IN AQUARIUS corresponds to the stability

♄ - ♒

aspect and the fixed-air sign Aquarius. This influence can only be manifested when the individual has made much progress, for in this sign the formative will if not renounced may do much harm, because Saturn is here the bridge between the will of the Higher Self and the Lower. To the awakened it gives the ability to judge character, to fix the attention, and to meditate on subjective or abstract thoughts. It is either a dumb note or one capable of blending with all other notes harmoniously.

♄ - ♓

SATURN IN PISCES corresponds to the harmonious aspect of the mutable-water sign Pisces. This is a dualistic influence and a very critical one. The man or woman under this influence may either be his own worst enemy, or suffer acutely through his enemies. It is truly the sign of self-undoing, for Saturn's influence, where the Self either yields the whole of the Will to higher powers or allows himself to become a medium and thus easily influenced or controlled by others. It promises deep sympathy, great love and unselfishness or else much depression, despondency, and an overbrooding nature. The will-power or desire-nature as the case may be, is rarely over strong, and the whole nature is too often paradoxical and difficult to understand. It favours those who grow through pain and seek self-realisation through responsiveness or an unselfish or unobtrusive life.

Aspects to Saturn

From these brief descriptions of Saturn's influence in the various signs, culled from actual first-hand experience, we may see the inclination which the influence of Saturn gives to each sign, modified however by the aspects Saturn receives from the other planets. By the aspects of the planets we very often obtain a clue to the real influence of Saturn.

♄ - ♆

When Saturn is in conjunction with the planet NEPTUNE we note a very curious influence affecting the subconscious mind, which makes those under its influence very psychic and receptive, and gives some eccentricity which takes the form of a peculiar bias toward certain things; sometimes it produces great deception, illusions and hypersensitiveness. Saturn in good aspect to Neptune often produces unique experiences in which the will is strengthened for good, and is a position which may lead to clairaudience. Saturn in affliction with Neptune seems to involve the character in entanglements of various kinds bringing strange limitations.

Neptune thus corresponds much more with the earthy than the airy influence of Saturn and tends to bring a very receptive condition.

Saturn with URANUS is much more hopeful, for Uranus is the crowning influence of Saturn. It is quite

♄-♅ in harmony with the facts to state that Uranus represents the Will freed from the Desire-aspect. Saturn's influence is closely allied to the Will, as we have shown; but it is the will that is not free, meaning the Will aspect that is still conditioned by circumstances, environments, etc. Uranus represents the Will that moves freely and unaffected by circumstances. A Uranian is an occultist, and this sums up the true expression of the Uranian influence, and we shall deal with this more fully later. Saturn in conjunction with Uranus denotes a strong will, and this must be the high water mark of intelligence *for the man who can respond to it;* but out of the thousands born at the time of the conjunction very few can respond to more than a fringe of its influence.

The good aspects of Saturn and Uranus strengthen the will and incline to the occult path. The adverse aspects seem to break up the formative will or desire nature and produce a contest between the individual and the personal will. Their tendency is to break up conventions and to incline the native to live towards a higher or less circumscribed law of life.

The effect of JUPITER upon Saturn is very dependent upon which of the two planets is stronger in the nativity. If the nature shows it, there

♄-♃ may be great meanness and an ungenerous spirit; but if the disposition is a good one, then justice would be tempered with mercy; it is wholly a question as to whether Saturn will absorb Jupiter or vice versâ. In one case of a man born under Sagittarius it caused him on one occasion, when his father was thought to be dying, to postpone going to see his father on receipt of the telegram announcing the fact, until the next day when an excursion train was available, in order to save a few shillings! More often than not the conjunction of Jupiter with Saturn causes Saturn to rob Jupiter of its virtues; but there are cases where the whole of the determination of Saturn takes on a religious colouring through the conjunction.

Saturn in good aspect with Jupiter is a very fortunate influence, giving either a philosophic or a practical religious tendency.

Saturn in affliction with Jupiter is however very unfortunate, bringing many social restrictions.

♄ - ♂

It is when we come to the MARS aspects to Saturn that we note a strange accentuation of the Saturnian influence. Mars in conjunction with Saturn may make a very strong character, and is a great asset in a man's life where the blending of feeling and mind is concerned; the desire nature is powerful for good or ill. If the horoscope is of the martian type, that is, if a martian sign rises or many planets are in martian signs, Mars will tend to absorb Saturn and strengthen the direction of the force; but in a Saturnian horoscope tact and diplomacy will be added to the force giving much tenacity and purpose,—and this reveals another phase of Saturn's influence, that of *tact* or *diplomacy.*

When Saturn and Mars are in good aspect to each other we often find a powerful character through the tempering of the hot and fiery Mars with the cold and restraining Saturn, and this tempering improves the direction of the Saturn influence.

We find the reverse of this when Saturn and Mars are in afflction; it is then often a hard fight between the emotions and the restraining power, and very often some undesirable traits of character are exhibited through its influence, in an undeveloped person; such as violent outbreaks of temper, and a tendency to use violence when enraged; and in general it tends to excite the passions. All persons under its influence are liable to become extremists for good or evil.

One of the finest illustrations of an evolved saturnian man, and a favourable expression of the influence of the planet Saturn upon a human being, is to be found in the horoscope of Mr. A. P. Sinnett, author of *Esoteric Buddhism, The Occult World, The Growth of the Soul*, etc., etc., who was born with his ruling planet Venus in conjunction with Saturn in the sign Sagittarius, and the third house, the house of the mind.

Illustrations

In this horoscope Saturn has absorbed a considerable amount of the virtues of the planet Venus and ***translated*** the conjoined influence, through the mutable and philosophic sign Sagittarius, into a practical expression of the higher or subjective mind represented by Venus.

x	xi	xii	i	ii	iii
♋ 18½	♌ 23	♍ 22	♎ 14	♏ 9	♐ 11

☉	☽	☿	♀	♂	♃	♄	♅	♆
♑ 28	♋ 27½	♑ 6½	♐ 14	♒ 22½	♏ 16	♐ 18	♓ 14	♒ 12

In summing up the horoscope in *The Art of Synthesis* we said: "Personality, positive, intellectual, philosophical, well-balanced; much dignity; good sympathy and humane tendencies.

"Capacity for public work, with love of retirement pulling against ambitious desires for intellectual service.

"Good social opportunities and much power quietly to influence others favourably. Long life, an honourable old age, and a reputation that will live long after his death. Sorrows through deaths and peculiar estrangements from friends."

The limitations of Saturn Mr. Sinnett has felt in a peculiar way, but he has gone far in spreading a profound knowledge of the realities of life. His horoscope is worthy of study so far as the planet Saturn is concerned. Students will notice that besides having his ruling planet in conjunction with Saturn in the sign of Saturn's exaltation, the Sun is in Capricorn, the night house of Saturn and Mars in Aquarius, the day house;

while the Moon is in the tenth house, corresponding to Saturn and Capricorn.

x	xi	xii	i	ii	iii
♋22½	♌27	♍26	♎17	♏13	♐15

☉	☽	☿	♀	♂	♃	♄	♅	♆
♑13½	♑29	♑1	♐9	♏16	♌6½r	♑11	♏26½	♐14

Another excellent illustration of the pure Saturnian type is the horoscope of Sir Isaac Pitman, the inventor of phonographic shorthand, born under the human sign Libra with the Sun in conjunction with the planet Saturn in the sign Capricorn, the negative house of Saturn.

x	xi	xii	i	ii	iii
♍22	♎20	♏9	♏24	♐26	♒10

☉	☽	☿	♀	♂	♃	♄	♅	♆
♐7	♐22½	♐9	♑22½	♐27	♍17	♏22	♓5	♒6

Probably the best example of a self made man born with the planet Saturn rising in conjunction with the ascendant is that of Sir William Allan, who rose from the ranks of a working engineer to a position of wealth and fame, and it is very characteristic of Saturn's influence that he should say he owed his rise to his own efforts and nothing to fortune. "The world has been my chief education" he said, "And men my books."

The influence of a weak and afflicting Saturn is given on page 228 of *The Art of Synthesis*, where other useful matter will also be found.

"ALCHEMY . . . is studied under three distinct aspects, which admit of many different interpretations, *viz.* the Cosmic, Human, and Terrestrial. These three methods were typified under the three alchemical properties—sulphur, mercury, and salt. Different writers have stated that there are three, seven, ten, and twelve processes respectively; but they are all agreed that there is but one object in alchemy, which is to transmute gross metals into pure gold. WHAT THAT GOLD, HOWEVER, REALLY IS, VERY FEW PEOPLE UNDERSTAND CORRECTLY. No doubt there is such a thing in nature as transmutation of the baser metals into the nobler, or gold. But this is only one aspect of alchemy, the terrestrial or purely material, for we sense logically the same process taking place in the bowels of the Earth.

"Yet, besides and beyond this interpretation, there is in alchemy a symbolical meaning, purely psychic and spiritual. While the Kabbalist-Alchemist seeks for the realisation of the former, the Occultist-Alchemist, spurning the gold of the mines, gives all his attention and directs his efforts only towards the transmutation of the baser *quaternary* into the divine upper *trinity* of man, which when finally blended are one.

"The spiritual, mental, psychic, and physical planes of human existence are in alchemy compared to the four elements, fire, air, water, and earth, and are each capable of a three-fold constitution, *i.e.* fixed, mutable, and volatile. Little or nothing is known by the world concerning the origin of this archaic branch of philosophy; but it is certain that it antedates the construction of any known zodiac, and, as dealing with the personified forces of nature, probably also any of the mythologies of the world."

H. P. BLAVATSKY, *Th. Glossary*, p. 15.

LECTURE III.

SYNOPSIS.—Saturn as the Master Builder—His relation to the Great Gods—the contrast between Saturn and other factors in human evolution—the evolution of Saturn as a type—Saturn and the Kabala—the Rays: Personal, Individual and Monadic. CONCLUSION: The Alchemy of Saturn—Transmutation.

☉ ... ♄

"*When the Sun and Saturn unite, then there is the true philosophical genius. The Sun awakens the vital spirits, and in all his operations he resembles God, for as God hath the cup of life and death in His hands, and by His sole power kills and restores, so likewise does the Sun bear a resemblance; for the Almighty does, as it were, look through into this world through the Sun, the local residence of the glorified humanity of Jesus Christ and the original paradise, and communicates his goodness by the light that is measured and proportioned to our capacity who are not able to look on his inexhaustible Light, for no man can see him and live.*"

♂ ... ♄ ... ♃

DESIRE, RESTRAINT, EQUILIBRIUM. These are three great steps in the pilgrimage of the Soul from innocence to enlightenment, and the ascent of each step is through the potent influence of the planets Mars,

Saturn and Jupiter; influences that are the reflections in the lower worlds of the powers emanating from the three great Gods Brahmā, Shiva and Vishnu, the energiser, regenerator and preserver of all manifesting things.

This is again mirrored for us in the signs of the zodiac. For instance Mars, the ruling planet of the sign Aries,

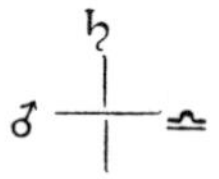

the first sign of the zodiac and the symbol of animal-man, is balanced in the opposite sign Libra, the day house of Venus. Saturn, the regenerating influence, ruler of the apex of the zodiac, the sign Capricorn, is exalted in the sign Libra. This is the Balance or human sign, in which spirit and matter are equally poised and it is truly said that a man reverses his spheres when he has humanised his permanent atoms to such an extent that all animal matter has been crushed out of his aura—symbolised by the planet Jupiter. The purer a man becomes the more potent also does the influence of Jupiter, the preserver, become in his life.

As we have already seen, the influence of the three planets Mars, Saturn and Jupiter, affects man's evolution in a very special manner.

Stimulation, Focalisation, Expansion

MARS seems to bring out man's latent qualities by an energising influence which tends to produce *action*. SATURN appears to establish relationship between the Ego and all that which goes to make up his environment, and is in this sense the planet of the "*I*"-*notion* making karma, fate or destiny. JUPITER builds up organic vehicles and finally organises the whole of the individual life into a perfect expression of the real self. MARS distributes an influence that is very active and stimulating in the *making* of temperament, and impels by impulse and desire. SATURN seems to decide the temperament through the relationship between the ego and its environment, (apart from forming its own special temperament within), which establishes the "I"-notion, making it stable and apparently permanent; it acts as the humanising influence and indicates a stage that is, so to speak, *between* the animal and the God in man. JUPITER organises, expands and increases the Ego's consciousness until it is ready to drop the separate "*I*"-*notion* and all sense of separateness and learn that it must expand to embrace the universe.

We seem in our deeper studies of astrology to be able to refer all the major influences affecting individuals to

♃

♂ ♄

these three important planets Mars, Saturn, and Jupiter; the two extremes of Mars and Saturn advancing human evolution by opposite tendencies, and the equalising influence of Jupiter ever striving to bring about the balance between these two extremes.

It may be that the Planetary Rays, concerning which there has been and is now so much curious interest, are

The Planetary Ray

related to these three planets in some very definite manner, such as the influence of the planet Mars over the purely Personal Ray, Saturn over the evolving Individual Ray and Jupiter over the Spiritual or what is known as the Monadic Essence. This only in the broadest sense.[11]

Astrologically we know very little about the particulars of these Rays, and although it seems quite clear that the Personal Ray should come from the sign rising at birth, the ruling planet, and the Moon, we know that it is quite possible for the ruling planet to absorb so much of the influence of the other planets as considerably to modify its influence. So that we cannot speak so definitely about the personal ray as to place it under any special planet in particular, although Mars is generally the most appropriate. In some cases a planet rising, if of a more ponderous nature than the ruler, will colour the whole life above and beyond all influence of the ruling planet. In only quite a general sense therefore is Mars the ruler of the Personal Ray, while the sub-influences of all the other planets modify or accentuate it.

Personal Ray

In the same manner Saturn is the nominal ruler over the Individual Ray but is again considerably modified or

---

[11] [The old astrologers wrote of Mars as governing the watery triplicity, Saturn the airy, and Jupiter the fiery.]

Individual Ray

accentuated by the Sun, Venus and Mercury, and by sub-influences of all the other planets. In addition to this however we may consider the planet Saturn as a *link* between the individual and the personal ray through its purifying and reasoning influence.

About the Monadic Ray we can know practically nothing and can only imagine that it is related to the higher attributes of the planet Jupiter, since this planet is undoubtedly connected with the Auric body in which we live and have our spiritual being.

Monadic Ray

We know by observations extended over many years, that the influence of the planet Mars is transmutable into that of Venus; but here it seems as though the influence of Saturn must in some way be concerned in this relationship between that of Mars and that of Venus as a refining and purifying agent. We are also led to believe that for the more advanced types of human beings the influence of Saturn is transmutable into that of Uranus, when the vehicles of consciousness are refined and purified to the state of physical perfection. With regard to Jupiter and Mercury, the influence of these planets seems to be interchangeable and to be particularly potent in the human evolution as distinct from the sub-human.

Transmuting Influences

In character building we may think of Saturn as the

The Master Builder

Master builder, using the influence of all the other planets as stones or material for his purpose. We know that each human character is the result of past experiences, the evolution of the ego being really the evolution of character, and this is represented in the details of each horoscope through which the Ego expresses itself. Thought as we know makes character; for thoughts repeated tend to produce acts, repeated acts become habit, and finally habit makes character. Astrologically we attribute persistent habits to the influence of the planet Saturn.

Temperaments

Now all *control of thought* seems to arise out of the influence of Saturn, the subduer. Whereas Mars, we find, gives rise to impulses towards action, and to attractions towards thought and action *through desire*. It is in this way we form our temperament; the martian temperament for instance arising out of impulses, the accentuation of desire, and the love of activity. And therefore for the MARTIAN TEMPERAMENT action is the key-note. For the MERCURIAL TEMPERAMENT, knowledge is the method; while the VENUS or ARTISTIC TEMPERAMENT is formed by the love of art, beauty and harmony. The JUPITERIAN TEMPERAMENT is cultivated by hope, religious feelings, charity and benevolence.

The SATURNIAN TEMPERAMENT in its earliest stages is often an unlovely one, owing to the endeavour that is made to balance the mind and emotions, and the slow and deliberate manner in which it is built; but it is made by silent resolve and endeavour, perseverance, industry and patience into a very permanent and enduring temperament, ultimately ending in a love and passion for truth, purity and serenity which win confidence and respect. All these tempering influences go to make up the rhythm of the geometrical figure of the nativity, and from it the music and aroma of every personality is produced.

The Secret of Saturn

The secret of Saturn's influence as the Master Builder of character is the strong tendency to duty and to responsibility which it gives, and we find the true saturnian person rarely shirking responsibility but ever attempting to accentuate it; that is to say, taking ever a higher and higher view of his responsibilities. This leads to the crown of Saturn's influence, which is the power to transmute, through the contemplative and meditative property of that planet, vices into virtues. For the key-note of his influence is that of *purifying* all that it contacts. The influence of Mars may be transmuted or changed through the regenerating influence of Saturn into the highest devotion, and that of Mercury into wisdom, and these are the two wings of the soul; but the alchemy of changing vice into virtue is essentially saturnian, and of Saturn's influence from the lowest to the highest it may be truly said—the greater the sinner the greater the saint, since Saturn evolves and raises man by the world's greatest teacher, experience. In a very particular sense the work of Saturn is that of the *regenerator*: and the method is by the conservation of energy and especially by that conservation which retains and conserves the vital fluids. It is the slow building of the vehicles for permanent use on higher planes which makes Saturn the friend of the yogi and ascetic; and to the influence of that mighty and far-reaching planetary sphere of Saturn we may trace every sacrifice of the lower to the higher mode of life.

Saturn's connection with the building of character was known to the ancients. According to the ancient astrologers there is in Saturn the property of contemplation, which is traced to an innate desire for all *secret wisdom and deep science*, and it was said of this planet that its influence "stirs up the contemplative faculty of man and kindles in him a desire to know the mysteries of God and nature; and this is done accordingly if the soul be good. But if the unlawful appetite of the fiery essence of the planet Mars prevail, then it seeks not the mysteries from God and nature, for it knoweth that a good life is required and that wisdom cometh from God, so that it despaireth to obtain the mysteries from God; and being unwilling to forsake sinful appetites it endeavours to obtain knowledge of the mysteries by unlawful means, and so

How the Ancients regarded Saturn

makes a bad use of the magical desire which was kindled in him by the Saturnian property."

Not "sad"

The Saturnian or saturnine temperament was not a "sad" one according to the ancient astrologers, but only serious, inclining to study, deep thought and a desire for solitude in order to contemplate and probe the mysteries; for they said that *the heart is the forge of the saturnian properties wherein the thoughts rise and are formed.* "As a man thinketh in his heart, so is he."

Saturn was not considered the planet of action but the builder of thoughts which prompt to action. In this sense Saturn is a centre of all true self-consciousness.

Another Standpoint

We may recapitulate our analysis of the three planets Mars, Saturn and Jupiter, by dealing with them from quite another standpoint, for the purpose of revealing more of Saturn's very subtle influence. For instance we may take the evolution of Saturn as a type alone by a new process of classification.

Self,—
Not-Self,—

The classification of man and the planets in terms of thought, feeling and action is fairly well known. Another and a larger grouping however seems to be demanded when we are considering Saturn, namely that of the Self, the Not-self, and the Relation between them. For practical purposes the Self is the man, the consciousness, using a physical body as a vehicle of expression in this physical world; and the Not-self is the whole of his surroundings, his environment, whether animate or inanimate, which acts upon him through his five senses, and upon which he reacts by means of his muscles and motor-organs. It is the body that brings these two, the Self and the Not-self, into relation with each other, and in so doing forms a concrete representation of that Relation. The Self is always within and hidden; the Not-self is always without and is not hidden; and the living body, with its various chemical and vital energies, serves the purpose of bringing these two into relation with each other, which would otherwise have remained disconnected and out of relation. His environment acts upon the man through the bodily senses, and the man reacts upon his environment through the muscles of the body.

—and the Relation between them

These are the outer and inner universes, the man within and the world without. In the first chapter of *The Art of Synthesis* it is pointed out that each planet is capable of being classified in these terms, and an account is there given of the meaning of each when stated in terms of consciousness within, of the world without, and of body, intermediate between the without and the within. It is difficult to give a complete description of the meaning of Saturn unless this classification is borne in mind.

Notice, however, that all the planets alike have an outward or centrifugal and an inward or centripetal tendency, as well as being capable of interpretation in terms of the balance or equipoise of the two. That is to say every planet's influence can be interpreted in terms of consciousness, the Self within, the centripetal tendency; again in terms of the outer world, the Not-self, the centrifugal tendency; and a third time in terms of the balance or relation or adjustment of these two. This applies to all alike and not to one only, but nevertheless any given planet has a greater affinity with one of these three modes than with another. For example, Mars has a greater tendency to go out into the world than to shut itself up in a state of contemplation or abstraction, whereas one of the tendencies of the Mercury man is to live too much in a world of thought and to become absent-minded and indifferent to the world without, although he also has his part and lot outside as well as other people. It will be necessary to discover the influence of each planet in terms of each of these three departments before we can claim to understand philosophical or Esoteric Astrology; and the occult classification of the subject will go further still, carrying us into inner or super-physical planes of existence.

Centrifugal and Centripetal

The life of Mars begins in sensation. Primitive man, in the early stages of his evolutionary pilgrimage, lives

Primitive Man

an almost purely animal life. In common with the animals, he realises that certain experiences yield pleasure and enjoyment, and he seeks these experiences and the objects associated with them over and over again, impulsively and without restraint. Sooner or later he learns that pain and disagreeable experiences are sometimes intermingled with the pleasure; and then he associates in his memory, more instinctively than deliberately, pleasure with one class of objects and pain with another class, the one to be sought and the other to be avoided. Any man who takes a dog for a walk in the country will find himself furnished with a useful object-lesson in the dog's behaviour, in its readiness to respond *instantly* to any new sensation, even while actually in quest of the gratification of a previously excited desire.

Pleasure and Pain

Here arises the first elementary distinction between Mars and Saturn. Mars rushes out in the pursuit of pleasure; and the evolution of the Mars man consists in learning the use and control of that strength which is implied in this outrush of impulsive energy. Saturn, on the other hand, begins its career in pain and in fear, in shrinking away from any objects that may possibly cause disagreeable experiences. Not that pain and Saturn are inseparable, for this is not the case; but until evolution has advanced very far, pain, whether of body or of mind, serves the purpose of drawing out—*educating*, in the real sense,— the Saturnian qualities of caution, prudence, self-restraint and self-control. The man finds, not only that certain objects generally yield an excess of pain over pleasure, but that even pleasure-giving objects may cause that form of disagreeable experience which we call satiety, when pursued too far. Such experiences are registered in the memory of the soul and are handed on from life to life, not as self-conscious recollection but as a kind of soul-instinct which is easily called forth at the sight of any object capable of appealing to it. Detailed objects and experiences are not remembered from one incarnation to another; neither those which yield pleasure and which call forth material qualities, nor those accompanied by pain, which teach the necessity for Saturnian caution. That which is actually incorporated in the soul and handed on to subsequent incarnations is, on the one hand, the ability to feel and to put forth the energy of pursuit, and, on the other hand, the ability to respond to warnings of danger and to put forth the energy of restraint and self-control.

These two contrasted faculties are built into the soul by repeated experiences in the outer world; and although

Innate Faculty

the separate objects and occasions that called them forth are forgotten, the faculties remain, and their presence in the man is shown by his quickly responding to comparatively slight experiences which call for their exercise, even in early childhood. At a very early age the Martian and Saturnian types are distinguishable, and even trifling events and happenings will prove that the soul has brought with it to rebirth ardour and enthusiasm or caution and restraint.

It may be remarked in passing that this also illustrates the evolution of conscience, the inner faculty which dictates, guides and warns. To a large extent conscience is associated with the Saturnian aspect of the mind, at any rate with that mode of conscience which is expressed in "Thou shalt not." This does not cover the whole subject, however, for in a larger sense each planet is associated with a type of inner experience which, when it is manifested outwardly as the voice from within comes under the general heading of conscience or duty. Thus Mars teaches courage and devotion to a cause as a conscientious duty; Mercury the duty of gaining and imparting wisdom; and so on, each after its own nature, each faculty speaking from experience gained in past lives.

Conscience

In the very early stages of evolution, conscience and the type of character are both alike—if not selfish, at least self-centred and egoistic. The warning of conscience runs something like this: "You must not do that; if you do you will suffer as you have suffered in the past": a self-centred but necessary piece of advice. The

Early Stages

character of primitive man as manifested in his everyday life is of a similar type: for even his attachment to wife, child or companion is largely conditioned by the fact that they increase his personal comfort; and if they fail to do this, or if they act adversely to what he considers his interests, the attachment will seldom stand the strain! Indeed the same is true even after evolution has advanced considerably; egoism comes first and altruism afterwards; brotherhood and unity cannot be realised until the separate selves are strong and self-reliant. So that nearly all the early development of the Saturnian type of character is rooted in self and turns upon considerations affecting self. The same is true of other types of character also: the earlier half (or more than half) of evolution is, if not selfish, at any rate self-centred. Conscience says very little about one's duty to one's neighbour in the early stages of the human career of the soul, while the ideal of loving one's neighbour as one's self is impossible of comprehension to the primitive soul. This is especially true of Saturn, a type closely associated with self all the way through its career. Beginning with selfish considerations, based upon advantages to be gained by the personal self, ideas of right and wrong are slowly built into the character of the soul. These ideas turn upon self in the early stages and later are expanded and generalised so as to include duty to others; while only in the latest stages of evolution is the idea entertained of impersonal duty to all beings alike. The Saturnian form of this ideal seems to be that of impersonal abstract justice; not justice in the popular distorted sense of severity and harshness, but a holding of the balance exactly even, and inclining neither to the one side nor to the other; the sense in which true justice and true mercy are one and the same.

The Drawbridge

The evolution of the Saturnian type of soul thus proceeds from the personal to the impersonal, and the idea of self is gradually expanded to include other selves within its scope. The duty of Saturn is to include these other selves while not losing touch with the separate individual self; to preserve the balance between the two tendencies, the altruistic and the egoistic; and to act as the bridge between the outer world of the Not-self,—which is really made up entirely of other selves, great or small—and the inner world of the Self.

From Concrete to Abstract

Another characteristic of the evolution of consciousness, and especially in the Saturnian type, is that it proceeds from the concrete and practical to the abstract and theoretical, and from that which moves almost entirely in the outer world of action and in the immediate present to that which realises its source in the inner world of thought and which ranges over the past and future as well as the present, "looks before and after" as Shelley says in contrasting man with the unself-conscious skylark. Those who have studied the influence of Saturn in human nature know that in the early stages and primitive types it reduces everything to matter-of-fact action and value in the outer world, and that it is of a rather slow-moving unimaginative, sordid, mean and practical character. It moves in the outer world; its interests are concrete and solid; it is slow to change, persevering and laborious in action, meaning to achieve its object whatever the trouble involved, though disliking needless effort; it is difficult to influence, persuade or modify; and its attention is given to the life of to-day and not to an ideal future in some land of dreams. We seem justified in supposing that the evolution of this type proceeds very slowly in its early stages. The accumulation of experience in the outer world, however, gives an increase of intelligence and of ideas stored in the soul; the horizon is widened and energy is accumulated; and inner character and will are more and more the guiding powers in the life. Abstract ideas are superimposed upon concrete experiences, and the man is rendered capable of moving more in a world of thought and becomes less the slave of the present day and its immediate interests.

Abstract predominating

This growth of the abstract at the expense of the concrete, and this increased predominance of the world of inner experience over that of the outer life, are seen in all departments of the character.

The inner world of thought becomes fuller and deeper, and exercises more control over the outer life; the feelings become more ideal and less dependent upon passing objects and experiences to awaken them; and the actions are to a greater extent guided by the deliberate will from within and less by momentary impulse. The characteristics here described, of course, are to a large extent common to all types of souls, and are not peculiar to those who are evolving under the influence of Saturn. In all alike the inner abstract thought, the inner ideal feelings, and the inner will are seen to grow and increase and finally to assume complete control over the outer life; and in all of them the inner world is brought into closer and closer touch with outer action.

Tamas, Rajas, Sattva

In the Saturnian type however there are certain characteristics that, so far as we know, remain to the last, and apparently serve to distinguish this from other types. Perhaps the most distinguishable of these characteristics is the quality of slowness, INERTIA. The three gunas or qualities inherent in matter as described in Indian philosophy are well known: *tamas*, inertia, changelessness; *rajas*, activity, mobility, change; and *sattva*, balance, rhythm, the neutral mean between the two. These are present, combined in various proportions, in all types of planetary influence; but in the case of Saturn *tamas* seems to preponderate. Those who belong to this type are slow to move but steadfast and unchanging in action when moved; in feeling they are faithful, enduring, unyielding, often selfish and cold, but steadfast and fixed; and in thought they show similar characteristics, concreteness, tenacity, slowness to accept new ideas and a steady adherence to old ones: (*Matt.* xxi, 28-32).

This peculiarity of inertia leads to various results, and one is that the sense of *self* is very strong. The more one soul is separated from others and the stronger the barriers are between them, the more will that soul be compelled to live its own life, think its own thoughts and evolve its own type of character; and this seems to be the effect which tamas has upon consciousness, or rather upon the vehicles in which consciousness is functioning. Tamas implies difficulty in changing, resistance of all tendencies to change coming from without, and therefore a rather fixed and unyielding centre in which the notion of self grows up slowly but surely and is very firmly implanted. Such a self is unadaptable, not easily modified, and very egoistic. In fact it seems probable that the first realisation of self-hood, "*I*-ness," is bestowed by Saturn in every case, even in those souls that are evolving under the influence of other planets, (for every planetary type includes all other types as sub-influences although its own predominates largely); it is Saturn that evolves ahamkara, egoity, whether as type or as sub-type.

The Self-sense

Another consequence of tamas is that what it gets it keeps. It is not easily influenced from without, and is consequently very inert and indolent in the early stages of evolution, but what it once receives and adapts to itself it clings to tenaciously, whether in terms of ideas, feelings, habits, or actual property; it is self-centred and also selfish. In a somewhat similar way, whether taken as a planetary or as a zodiacal type, that which is characterised by inertia, becomes a rich centre, accumulation, or reservoir of that which is accumulated. Hence in the physical body Saturn is said to conserve vitality although not actually to produce it. Subjectively it conserves feeling and thought, and therefore gives a tenacious memory and power of concentration. The way in which Saturn as a type accumulates and clings to property and possessions is well known to students.

To Have and to Hold

No centre, however, can receive and accumulate indefinitely without giving out again. For every action, there is a reaction; and whenever any impact or stimulus is received, whether by body or mind, a reaction takes place and energy flows outwardly, moving the muscles and ending in action. Here Saturn is regarded as allied to the will, but will of the steady and persistent type, not the impulsive fiery will which acts quickly and ceases quickly and is characterised by changefulness—rajas. Action is the outer measure and manifestation of will,

Restraint

the test of what it can accomplish; but here, as in the other departments of consciousness there is not only an outer but also an inner aspect. Outer action is will in outward manifestation, the production of effects in the outer world; doing things. Inner action is the production of results in the worlds of feeling and of thought, which effects do not flow outwardly into the physical world, except in what may be called negative action, restraint of action. When a man strikes a hasty blow because of a passing impulse of anger, he is causing positive action based upon an outward-flowing emotion; but if Saturnian fear or deliberation intervenes and restrains the action, little or no outward effect may be produced other than the expression of the emotion in the features or in the modified heart-beat or the rate of breathing; and yet this restraint is a *real effect*, a negative action emotionally. Similarly mental concentration, "the hindering of the modifications of the thinking principle," is a real effect in the mental world although its physical result is relative quiescence rather than action.

Here we have three characteristics of the Saturnian type; self, will and action. But when we examine them closely, two things are to be noticed.

The Lower Self—

First, all three are of the slow-moving tamasic quality, as distinguished from other manifestations such as those of Mars which seem to be dominated by rajas, activity.

Second, which is perhaps only a natural result of the first, none of the three is perfect. Saturn gives us the notion of self; but it is probable that this is only the rudimentary personal self, and that the larger individual self requires the assistance of Uranus for its evolution; while the one cosmic self belongs to the Sun and not to any one planet alone. And similarly with regard to both will and action; if Saturn evolves the personal will of a slow-moving tamasic kind, Mars gives the swift-impulse will of the rajasic kind; Uranus the fully individualised will; and the Sun the one cosmic will.

This may perhaps be generalised by saying that Saturn signifies, or evolves, a relatively smaller personal centre of self, stated in terms of will

—and the Higher

or action, which is intended to be merged in or expanded into a larger individual or cosmic Self. This first small germ of self, which begins to manifest in the higher animals, and which even in them shows the customary three aspects of thought, feeling and action, is that which in man descends from the permanent individuality into the physical personality at each rebirth and which re-ascends out of it again at the death of the body and is then sooner or later merged again in the larger individuality from which it had its origin. It is therefore the link or bridge between the small and more restricted self of the personality, with its three aspects of personal thought, personal feeling, and personal action and the larger self of the individuality with its three similar but sublimer and more glorious aspects. Saturn is in this sense both the Sower and the Reaper of the harvest of the temporary personality, garnered by the immortal individuality. Its quality of tamas renders permanent that which would otherwise be only temporary, and holds in equilibrium the powers of the personal self for the benefit of the individual self.

The Basis of Personality

We have now sufficient material to assist us to understand the basis of personality from an astrological standpoint. Mars is stated to be an unconscious sower of the seeds of personal attachment through feelings drawn from the centre of the emotional soul by desire for expression in sensation or sentiment, or by attraction to objects that awaken the emotions, or by an ardent passion moving from within towards something without. Saturn, on the other hand, causes the mind to restrain itself, and tends to limit the expression either through fear or through the recollection of some painful experience in the past; and it therefore tends to *reap* the effects of past causes started by the impulses of the martian temperament, and also tends to sow fresh causes for future realisation under stronger saturnian vibrations in the future. It is clear, from all the statements that have been made in these two special courses of lectures, that Mars and Saturn are extreme influences connected with our personal development and that they act in opposite directions to obtain the same end, a complete personality. These two important planets are respectively related to the eastern angle of the horizontal line, or the Ascendant, and the apex of the perpendicular line or Midheaven. At the nadir the Moon rules, and its influence culminates in the point governed by Saturn. At the ascendant Mars rules and its influence is opposite to that of Venus ruling the western angle. These angles ruled by the Moon, Mars, Saturn and Venus form the cross of the Lower Quaternary, of the personality, which is constituted of:

> the gross matter of the body moulded over the etheric double—the earth, Carbon;
> the life or active power—the Sun, Oxygen;
> the etheric double on which the physical body is moulded—the Moon, Nitrogen; and
> the astral or desire nature of the animal man—Mars, Hydrogen.

The Cross holds the gross matter together and forms the physical body of animals and men. The Half Circle represents the etheric double, or the mould in which the gross matter is held during the personal life. The life principle or vital power animating the cross and half circle is symbolised by the Circle round the cross. The desire impelling it to action and motion is governed by the planets Mars and Saturn, or the two extremes of influence coming from them; the outrushing energy or desire of Mars being forced in upon itself by the limitations and restrictions of Saturn—♂ or ♁ and ♄ or ♄.

The Cardinal Cross shows the greatest activity of the personality, when all the forces are manifested in an active physical life. It is composed of the elements of Fire, Earth, Air and Water in conflict, as represented in the squares and oppositions of the angles; but as each element is a triplicity in itself, the cross or conflict has to be harmonised on each plane of being represented by these triplicities.[12] The interlacing of the triplicities in the zodiacal circle represents the concords and the conflict of those harmonies on the cross of life, in which the gunas play their part, represents the discords from which man has to make his own harmony. Kabalistic Astrology represents the idea of the triangles and the square in the accompanying illustration (p. 98).

The Triangles and The Square

We have spoken of Saturn as the Bridge between the higher and the lower. In the true Kabalistic or Hebrew Astrology Ye-sod represents the generative organs and means the foundation. It is the creative power thrown downward and is the great nature planet. The earth's zodiac, and the horoscope of a man, is but the mirror of the immortal man behind. Space and time as abstractions are

Foundation

---

[12] Earth, physical; Water, astral; Fire, mental; Air, spiritual.

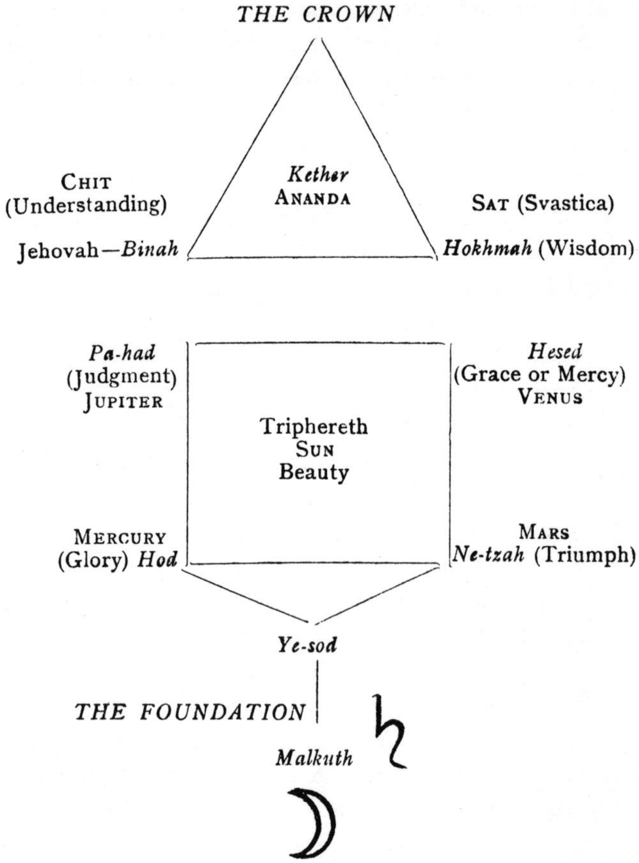
THE CROWN
Kether
ANANDA
CHIT
(Understanding)
Jehovah—Binah
SAT (Svastica)
Hokhmah (Wisdom)
Pa-had
(Judgment)
JUPITER
Hesed
(Grace or Mercy)
VENUS
Triphereth
SUN
Beauty
MERCURY
(Glory) Hod
MARS
Ne-tzah (Triumph)
Ye-sod
THE FOUNDATION
Malkuth

symbolised astrologically by Jupiter and Saturn; they are really one, but we see them under the limitations imposed upon them by our personal life. Step out of time or limitation into eternity and we are individual rather than personal. The Personality is but the mask we wear during the great play; yet it is not the part we play on the great stage of the world's drama that matters, but *how we play it.* We say that Saturn's metal is lead; we may use the lead of Saturn to make our mark in the world, and it will be the merit or VALUE of that mark which decides whether it shall endure or not. Metaphorically speaking we plunge the essence of our individual ego into the smooth lake of physical existence; it is not the plunge that counts of itself but the force we bring as character which makes ripples or circles upon the lake, and which affects the waters of life into which we plunge. Astrologically we shall not go far wrong in regarding the influence of the planet Mars as the Counterfeit of the Spirit, which *triumphs* over matter in the end by quickening the real self within us; and in regarding Saturn as the Shadow of the Substance.

Life, and Form

We may trace the animating principle or Kama from its lowest expression on the life side to the highest devotion a man can reach through the transmutation of the planet Mars, the emotional soul, which is in very truth the quickener of the spiritual as well as the quickener of the life during pregnancy.

We may also trace the long bridge of shadow and substance, which reaches from the etheric mould upon which the physical is modelled to that portion of the Aura which surrounds us all and which is connected with the true individual self. Saturn is a mystery truly, and none but the pure in heart may hope to solve its final problem. It is the foundation in more senses than one, for it is the builder of our forms from the mineral atoms to the perfect man.

The Pentagon

We may illustrate our Kabalistic ideas of Astrology in the symbol of the Pentagon, the *Star of Man.*[13] The "malefics" are at the base or the two feet of the man, the "benefics" are on the arms outstretched and the mutable planet Mercury at the apex. We are told by the Wise Man to "seek the way by retreating within"; and also to "seek the way by advancing boldly without." These are the two ways to salvation from the narrow limitations of the personal self. To each temperament there is a way which seems the most desirable: to the Mars man the road ends in devotion after ardent progress, to the Saturn man the road passes through contemplation and ends in self-sacrifice. BUT THE WAY IS NOT BY DEVOTION ALONE NOR BY CONTEMPLATION ALONE.

---

[13] Take a regular pentagon: from the extremity of one of its sides draw a line to the extremity of the side *opposite*, and continue the process until the starting point is regained. Erase the original five lines forming the pentagon, and you have the Five-Pointed Star.

Strange as it may sound, all the deeper students are agreed that the steps on the great ladder of life are the vices which are surmounted by the strength of Mars and the experience of Saturn. The virtues of these planets may also be necessary but *they alone* are not sufficient to reveal the truth which Astrology reveals that each man is HIMSELF absolutely the way, the truth and the life. "Thou canst not tread that path until thou hast thyself become that path."

The Man in the Street

The ordinary man of the world is mainly influenced by the force he draws from Mars and Saturn for his own personal use, and is therefore either unconsciously or cynically selfish; and all his efforts are concentrated upon his own self advancement, through his mind and senses turned to selfish ends being directed to obtaining the best for himself out of his physical life. And it is not until the sense of duty, responsibility and seriousness comes upon him that he contemplates the world apart from himself. The ordinary Mars man is greatly concerned in gratifying his appetites and obtaining all the pleasure he can out of his senses, and it is not until he substitutes the law of love for the law of self that he awakens to the fact that the world does not exist for him alone but also for his mother, his wife, and his children—and also for other men's mothers, wives and children.

We have all to pass through the three great halls of

instruction before we can find our way to freedom. The first is called the Hall of Ignorance or the world of sense and fluctuating moods or sensations under the influence of the Moon. The second is the Hall of Learning where the fruits of life are found to contain bitterness as well as sweetness; it is under the influence of Mars. The third is the Hall of Wisdom gained by experience, and it is there that the Master is to be found; it is under the influence of Saturn, and finally leads to the Guru or teacher under the influence of the greater fortune Jupiter. It is in the purification of the mind that we find Saturn's powerful influence and it is when we have learned to work for work's sake, to live in the eternal instead of being bound by time, and have found out how to grow in the silence that the ending of Saturn's influence is seen. We must then desire only that which is within us, and that which is beyond us, or as is so well expressed by the Wise Man "desire only that which is unattainable." It is not until then that we know our soul to be immortal, undying and eternal.

The Three Halls

This thought brings up the very necessary idea of reincarnation, the only theory that explains rationally the difference in organism, environment, social position, wealth, mental calibre, moral capacity and worldly circumstances, etc. With this theory before us we can under-

Reincarnation

stand the law of fate and fortune or Karma which shows us why the soul brings with it certain mental faculties and moral tendencies. For the law of Karma is the law of Cause and Effect, under the influence of Saturn and Jupiter. Each soul brings with it what has been worked for in the past, and each soul is now reaping under the justice of Saturn the harvest of its own sowing.

Question how we may, the evidence in favour of re-incarnation is too strong for us to reject. Why did Sir

Why . . . ?

William Hamilton at the age of 13 know 13 different languages when it takes an ordinary man several years to learn a single one of these languages?

Why . . . ?

Why should Mozart show in early childhood musical powers that many of us cannot hope to obtain after life-long work?

To take a personal case, which should be most convincing to astrological students. Why should it be

Why . . . ?

considered a 'gift' for the writer to take to astrology with ease without any previous study, a subject that is known to tax the keenest intellect—if he had not studied the subject closely in former lives? It is no credit to this poor brain which is entirely a new instrument in the present life, but to the Saturnian quality of intellect which gives industry, perseverance and painstaking labour, the result of hard work in former lives, now seen in the expression of ideas that come from the working of a law that is *within* and not without. It is Saturn's influence in every horoscope which reveals the Karma of the reincarnating ego, and with this knowledge before us we may find the way to freedom and liberation, where the bondage of time is changed for the freedom of the eternal life.

The "Ring-Pass-Not"

We think of the solar system as our universe, in which we live and move and have our being. The boundary line of that system, for us, is controlled by the ringèd Saturn the Guardian of those souls evolving in the system. In this sense he is the adversary, Satan and Chronos—Old Father Time. He is the great angel of Stability, and the perfect balancer of all forces, good and so-called evil, or positive and negative, spirit and matter. It is Saturn who is the Alpha and the Omega, the beginning and the end of time; and of him it is said, "Among the Gods is none like unto him, into whose hand are committed the Kingdoms, the power and the glory of the worlds. . . . . Many names hath God given him, names of mystery, secret and terrible. God calleth him Satan the adversary, because matter opposeth spirit, and time accuseth even the saints of the Lord." "For Satan is the magistrate of the justice of God; he beareth the balance and the sword. . . . . Therefore Satan is the Minister of God, Lord of the seven mansions of Hades, the angles of the manifested worlds." Many are the wonderful stories told of Saturn in the scriptures and elsewhere, but he has always been identified with Jehovah on high and represented by Moses, the law giver, on earth.

The Law Giver

Those who have passed through the pain of mind produced by the notion that God is capable of inflicting *everlasting punishment* on souls who are ignorant concerning the law of life will gladly welcome the idea that all the symbols connected with Saturn are those which describe the various aspects of the law-giver; and when the truth is realised that the law is absolutely just, confidence may be regained by the knowledge that no soul can be lost who is capable of redemption. It is only those who have so hardened their hearts that even Saturn cannot subdue them through time, who are doomed to wrestle finally with Saturn and know that every soul is destined by sacrifice to become perfect in the end.

Conservation of Energy

In concluding this course of lectures on the planet Saturn we feel conscious that very little has been said in comparison with what could be said concerning the secret of Saturn, who in very truth is the Reaper of the souls of men, and it may be well perhaps to dwell for a few moments on the secret that is revealed through transmutation. Many students of Astrology have remarked on the resemblance of the symbol of

Saturn to a serpent, and in many instances it has been suggestive of the serpentine power which every man possesses. The seed of life must neither be dormant and sterile nor wasted and abused, and the greatest secret Saturn's influence can teach humanity is the conservation of energy, how to conserve the seed and preserve it from decay, and yet transmute its force from generation to creation. This secret is learned through purity of thought, and the substitution of love for affection. We are too often affected by the feelings and impressions of others and falsely think we are of a loving disposition because the *affection* produces pleasure. Love is a force that comes from within ourselves and is foreign to all such terms as sensation, passion, or even patriotism. Shakespeare understood the difference between affection and love when he wrote:

> My king is tangled in affection to
> A creature of the Queen's, Lady Anne Bullene.
>
> (*King Henry VIII*. iii, 2.)

Love is the gift of the spirit and wants nothing but—to love. And when true love comes, Saturn's work is ended.

The Secret of Saturn

Finally the secret of Saturn is to turn desire into will, the will to be that which it is God's will you should seek to be. God leaves it to Saturn to restrain, for He restrains none, and is always waiting to receive those whom Saturn passes into the Kingdom of Heaven. Lest there should be any mistake that asceticism is right or isolation necessary, we may learn from the wise men of the East how they viewed emancipation through Saturn's influence. Yagna is a word used in the east, meaning sacrifice, and they taught that a householder, even if he had a large family to support, or many calls upon his resources, could find a friend in Saturn through sacrifice. They said that no matter what a man's calling or position in life might be, whether husband or lover, merchant or patriot, householder, artist, or working man, he might quickly find redemption through sacrifice. It was held by them that a man who could become oblivious of his own personality and wanted but little in this world might become the greatest of all *Yogis,*—that is, a man is law unto himself and at the same time law unto all other creatures of God. Such a man being a law unto himself might even dictate law unto death, who is Saturn, the great Law-Giver in the three worlds. For over the man who is truly law unto himself Saturn has no further power; for man is made in the image of God, and stripped of everything a man possesses he is a "divine fragment" of God's life, light and love. To yield the passing wants of the manifested world, to take what the world brings you contentedly, knowing that everything that is not of the spirit will pass away, is the sure road to that sacrifice which is the last with which the influence of Saturn can wrestle; for sacrifice is the surrender of all things material, and the destruction of that greatest of all heresies—the "heresy of separateness."

Sacrifice

There is the sacrifice of the senses and personal gratification, which may be burnt up and consumed in the purifying flame of Love; the sacrifice of the lower and limited mind, with its constant personal equation, which is illuminated through sacrifice by the light of Wisdom, which sees all souls around the great circumference of the material world being drawn to the centre of spirit by innumerable ways through God's wisdom; finally the sacrifice of all desire for personal fame or recognition, but with the will polarised to the spirit transmuting all desires into the one will which is to be one with the will of God. This is the severing of the bonds and limitations of Saturn, and none rejoices more than this great and mighty angel when a soul is pure enough to pass on beyond his ringed sphere into the boundless ocean of divinity.

A Constant Memory

Let him who desires to tread the path leading to liberation begin by saying the little text to be read on Sir Robert Peel's monument "My wealth consists not in the abundance of my riches, but in the fewness of my wants," and only adding to it the one want—a constant memory of God.